Counselling in Secondary Schools

By the same author

TEACHERS AS COUNSELLORS

ALICK HOLDEN

Counselling in Secondary Schools

WITH SPECIAL REFERENCE TO
AUTHORITY AND REFERRAL

CONSTABLE LONDON

Published by Constable and Company Limited
10 Orange Street, London WC2H 7EG
Copyright © 1971 by Alick Holden
All rights reserved
ISBN 0 09 457650 5

Set in Monotype Baskerville
Printed in Great Britain by The Anchor Press Ltd,
and bound by Wm. Brendon & Son Ltd,
both of Tiptree, Essex

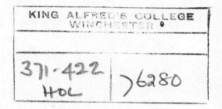

To students
past and present of
Hillfoot Hey High School
in Liverpool

Acknowledgements

To my wife and family I owe more than I can possibly express. If at times they must have felt like those of whom it was written 'They also serve who only stand and wait' it is they who have provided me with that continuing affection, care and concern without which no study of human relationships is possible. To Miss Sheelah Browne I am especially indebted, not only for typing the manuscript from an almost indecipherable mass of notes with inexhaustible patience and interest, but also for her abundant constructive comment and professional guidance. To Miss Elfreda Powell I am also grateful for her many helpful suggestions. Above all perhaps I thank those young people, who must remain anonymous, who appear to have seen me as a person fit to confide in, and from whom I have begun to learn how teacher-pupil relationships can be changed to the benefit of both parties. Lastly I must record my appreciation of the interest and understanding with which so many teaching colleagues have regarded my methods.

Contents

CONTENTS

Introduction

This book is a consequence of the further experience, discussion and thought which have ensued since the publication, two years ago, of my first book, *Teachers as Counsellors*. The latter was based upon case-histories and directed to the concept that teachers can be counsellors in their own schools given appropriate training after a selection process. This concept raises certain problems and a further study of some of these now seems to be a necessity. The present volume is intended to meet this need, and provides a more detailed treatment of three specific issues which seem to loom large in the minds of those with whom I have discussed counselling in the past two years. These are the teacher-counsellor's dual or triple role, the nature of school authority and the counsellor's relation to it, and the managerial or procedural problems of counselling when it involves consultation with or referral to supporting agencies. This volume is therefore intended to be a companion to the first, not a substitute for it: and in general it does not repeat what was in the first. If I appear to have dealt with certain topics rather cursorily in succeeding pages, this is because they were considered at some length in my first book.

My approach to these specific problems is, I believe, down-to-earth and practical, reflecting my own views and experience, and facing the questions which have been put to me by many teachers in various parts of the country. It is that of an experienced senior schoolmaster who has an immense faith in young

people, but who has had to look – and is still looking – hard
and long at the problems he is discussing, who has had to live
with the stresses these problems have created – and are
creating – in the constantly changing social milieu in which
a modern education service operates, who has had to accept
the fact that to some problems in counselling there are no
immediate or actionable solutions, who has experienced the
support, sympathy and interest of some members of the
teaching profession, as well as the downright rejection, incredulity or even hostility of others, and who accepts these views
and feelings as part of the situation in which any counsellor has
to practise his particular brand of relational and personal
therapy. No one, least of all a counsellor, should expect
immediate acceptance of new and revolutionary ideas, or
instant transformation among the doubters.

The attention I shall pay to the problems and practicalities,
as they urge themselves upon us with the vigour with which
all difficulties present themselves, should not blind us to what
lies behind my treatment of them, and to what this book is
really about. It is about people. For this very reason it is at
times intensely personal, since it cannot escape reflecting the
intensity of my own feelings about the unhappiness and
frustration, the helplessness and anger, in young clients who are
entitled to a better example and understanding than the
adult world and the educational service at present offer them.
In passing, this is not to say that they are blameless for what we
term their misdemeanours – they are not – but to argue this
matter is not my purpose here. This book is about the hopes
and resources some have generated as they sat and talked
nervously with me and the disappointment that others have
carried sadly out of my room, perhaps because of my inadequacy to bolster their failing resolution. It is about my halting
and feeble attempts to perceive the conflicts within them, and
my inability to see the world through their bright uncompro-
mising eyes rather than the sombre and sometimes compro-
mising vision of middle age. It is about the fleeting privilege

of seeing a young man summon up the courage to face his failings, or to pick himself up after falling at one hurdle in life and go for the next one with renewed vigour as he draws on hitherto unrealized resources in his personality, or begins to develop a new one. It is concerned with my feelings, as a schoolmaster, about the stress and anxiety, the fascination and humility which the dual and triple roles bring in their train. It is about the fact that I can never meet a client or a class now, and ever be the same person again: and hence it is about the searing challenges which counselling offers to my character and motives as well as my philosophy of education.

I know well enough that feelings are not a substitute for the cool objectivity of clinical research. But the latter would be difficult enough in all conscience, particularly at the relatively unsophisticated level at which counsellors work in school. Yet even the laconic and dispassionate reports of clinicians use words to describe their findings, just as I try to use them to describe my feelings. Yet neither form of words can adequately convey to an intending novice of counselling precisely what counselling is, because it is an abstraction until a person is actually involved in it. It cannot be held up or shown off, like an apple, to illustrate the meaning of the word 'apple'. Thus the range of variation in interpreting the word counselling is wide. Of course, we can use tape-recorders, written case-histories, even film, and say 'That is counselling.' But everyone observing such recorded demonstrations will interpret them differently because his feelings and habits, prejudices and experience affect his reactions to something novel, because he is human. Thus mere words limit our understanding of client-counsellor relationships, each of which is itself unique. Moreover, descriptions devoid of feelings fail to convey the sense of wonder, surprise and humility evoked by the change for the better which can occur in a client's character: a change which seemingly comes from within himself because his counsellor is not, and perhaps cannot be, aware of the part he has played in the transformation, other than that in some vague way his relationship with the client contributed to the metamorphosis.

So when we strip off the practical problems of counselling, its relationship with authority, the complexities of the dual and triple roles, the organization of referral – when we have peeled this outer skin away – the delicacy of the relationship, the subtle interplay of personalities and the possible emergence of what seems to be a new character in the client remain. This is something to marvel at. Of course we must be as objective as we can, and involve all the resources of science and social service as we need them: we must also deal, as I try to, with the problems people pose; but if we cease to marvel, then as human beings we are lost. Thus the insertion of my own feelings, even when I ask the questions which this book asks, may be helpful to some who contemplate involving themselves in the form of therapy we call counselling, and remind them that it is people with whom counsellors are concerned. For even management problems, counselling apart, are about human beings and the relationship between them. Yet far too many teachers give a very good impression of being over-concerned about organization statistics, and systemization of counselling in schools rather than with the human problems of student clients and the challenges to counsellors' character and person-alities which these problems make. I have formed much the same impression about the conceptualization of counselling, or its intellectualization. Systems and ideas, in this field of human relationships, should be secondary to the needs of people. In a remarkable broadcast in the B.B.C. 'Viewpoint' series, Richard Hoggart, Assistant Director-General of UNESCO, observed that the English have always done one thing rather well, and that is to think in human and humane terms rather than in purely intellectual or organizational. It seems to me that our contribution to counselling in schools should reflect this national virtue and not be excessively concerned with its machinery or intellectual concepts.

After a brief description of the setting for counselling, I give a short account of some aspects of counselling, including its relationship with the pastoral care and social welfare activities which so many teachers seem to think are the same as counselling. An analysis follows of the so-called dual role of the teacher-counsellor and the distinguishable triple role of the senior teacher who counsels. I then discuss the make-up of school authority and control, consider the relevance and value of its various conventional components in the 1970's, and invite teachers seriously to think about why they do so many of the things which so many of them still believe are important for maintaining authority in schools. For there are still many people who believe that counselling erodes authority: this is an erroneous conception. I then consider the relation between counselling and certain social educational agencies, together with the managerial problems of referring your clients to them. I hope that this will not only help teachers but also improve communication between schools and these agencies and thus dispel some of the lingering suspicion which exists between them.

I hope that my approach to these practical problems will commend itself to teachers of all ages who are interested in re-directing our educational effort towards personal and moral goals and away from those which are principally intellectual and vocational, and to those who are much interested in the education service's structural or managerial problems. Administrators, governors, parents, social workers, staffs of colleges, polytechnics and universities may find it useful. Its foundation is mainly experience and conversation in private with real young people, seventy-five per cent of whom had no history of family education beyond the age of fifteen, and who were in many cases pushing forward into new worlds of knowledge and experience without support from their families. The latter had none to give. In that foundation, however, must also be included the views of teachers of all ages whose training is largely conventional, often unimaginative, and sometimes utterly irrelevant. Their opinions and experience, whether they were for or against my views, I respect and value as an inescapable part of the environment in which any counsellor must work.

Teachers, perhaps more than any other part of the population, tend to cling to what is familiar to them when they are confronted with the unknown and the unfamiliar. Thus the penultimate chapter may reassure some of them, for in it I have adduced evidence from the history of the philosophy of education to show that the approach and attitudes of the teacher-counsellor are not quite as new-fangled as opponents and sceptics seem to think they are. Modern views about the psychological needs of people and the demands made by new curricular techniques only buttress ideas which have long been in the minds of educational philosophers. Thus, as well as dealing with the practicalities and stresses – latent or real – of counselling by teachers, I hope I have also provided some part of a philosophical basis for counselling by teachers in their own schools. Such people need such a basis as much as anyone else who performs a service for other human beings, and probably much more so.

A further point is pertinent. This book, like *Teachers as Counsellors* has an English context. Its argument however is not necessarily restricted to any particular national situation, philosophy or culture. For although each society has its own special educational system and traditions, the discussion herein is about students and their relationships with teachers the problems and difficulties of which I suspect have much in common the world over, even allowing for differences of nationality, race, religion, and philosophy. It may be argued that my thinking is the product of an educational system and a nation at a particular stage of social development, a stage at which it is compelled to look at new relationships in education as well as other fields of social action. This may well be true: but it is equally true that the world as a whole is changing so rapidly and communicating so effectively, thanks to modern technology, that other national and racial cultures may find themselves confronted with the sort of situations which counselling and related methods may be used to deal with effectively in this country. The need to recognize the value of individuals is international. Moreover the philosophical background to counselling has a notable international flavour about it. Thus my thesis should not be regarded as one which is necessarily valid only for the current stage of social and educational evolution in the United Kingdom, but as one which is in itself universal, sensible, humane, workable and desirable, because it is basically a part of the brotherhood of man which links generations as well as nations and races. The need for that link of generations is common to all cultures.

Lastly there is a suggested list of texts for further reading. This is not exhaustive, but I have found them stimulating and I believe that those who wish to pursue the matter further will find them equally helpful.

I

The setting

A century of compulsory education has brought two interesting developments in its train. The first is a growing revolt against the repressiveness and narrowness of much traditional secondary education, and its continuing, even extending, preoccupation with examinations as a measure of total educational success. The second is a complementary but more positive movement towards educating the student's whole person, instead of just enhancing his intellectual capacity. Conceivably, the first is a sign that the second has not developed fast or far enough, that the movement has not become generally established practice. There is an accompanying implication that when schools and colleges pay attention to the second movement the first revolt does not occur. Counselling is one of the ways by which we may satisfy the broader personal educational needs of students in schools, and indeed in establishments of further and higher education. Although it is not the only way, of all the changes in method and approach which mark the present stage of educational evolution, the technique of the counsellor is potentially the most revolutionary when it is compared with the conventional role and practice of the traditional teacher. For counselling, either with a single individual or with small groups of students, calls, as we shall see, for teachers to abandon their traditional authority and to accept their student clients as they are, without any reservations whatsoever, and in absolute privacy. Under these conditions, the counsellor – and I am dealing in this book with the teacher-counsellor – must adopt the same approach as the non-teaching specialist counsellor and face his youthful client in a relationship of equality and partnership. The stress of this situation can mainly be borne and mitigated by the inner resources of the counsellor's own personality and ethos, not by the authority implicit in his position or by an arbitrary system of punishment. This is not to say that he has no authority at all – we shall come to this matter in more detail later – but whatever authority he possesses in this new counselling role is attributed to him by his clients as distinct from being imposed on them by him. Why they should thus attribute it is a matter for them. This alone makes it different, and it certainly is not – and does not need to be – enforceable by any system of legal sanctions.

Such a revolution in student-teacher relationships appears to strike hard at the very roots of school authority and discipline, certainly in Britain and western Europe where the authority of the teacher in his classroom and outside, has for long been traditionally absolute and effectively beyond any appeal against it. It is true that spasmodic violence and growing indiscipline in schools in tough areas of large towns and cities constitute a challenge to this absolute view of the teacher's role, and a challenge reinforced by the disinterest or hostility of a minority of parents. None the less this is a special problem which demands special treatment through a variety of social agencies, in addition to purely educational action, and it does not invalidate the general criticism that the unchallengeable authority of teachers is now an educational anachronism. The recollection of such arbitrary and absolute authority is probably the cause of much parental diffidence, fear and hostility where their relations with teachers are concerned. And, despite many teachers' belief to the contrary, these aspects of their authority still persist in many schools even in these enlightened days. By contrast with the situation in the British Isles, a tradition of personal independence and individual freedom in the United States, and to a lesser extent in the English-speaking former Dominions, may have stifled the growth of such an autocratic image of the teacher and the consequent inequality in relationships between teacher and taught. It is interesting in this connection that counselling in schools has received far more attention in the United States than anywhere else, although critics may point to reports of total breakdown in some American schools as vicarious evidence of the risks inherent in a non-autocratic teacher position. Be this as it may the counselling situation, in the terms in which I describe it, provokes in the minds of teachers in this country, and in those of others involved in the educational service, serious misgivings about its effect upon school authority and discipline. They foresee also some difficulty in relating it to social and welfare services which already exist and function well. In addition they see a further complication of school management. Added to the usual problems of managing staff and curriculum are those of fitting the radical process of counselling into the already complex nexus of normal school relationships. At worst, those who have misgivings about counselling envisage the possible total destruction of the framework of authority and discipline upon which they believe a school depends for its successful operation, so that it becomes unmanageable. At best they foresee that the introduction of counselling techniques will create major conflicts of loyalty between those of the counsellor and his client on the one hand, and on the other the loyalties of both to traditional school ethos and to staff and student allegiances. It has also been suggested to me that such conflicts, contravening as they do the general principle that no man can serve two masters, may create in the minds of both counsellor and client serious dilemmas, culminating in some cases in serious mental distress. They might also conceivably spread some as yet undefined alarm and despondency among members of staffs who expect traditional obedience from students and professional loyalty among their teaching colleagues. As far as relationships with social welfare organizations are concerned, their present great merit is that serious home difficulties and moral problems can be handled confidently by them without any risk that private details about pupils homes will circulate freely round their schools. The privacy of homes is sacrosanct, however deprived and squalid they may appear to be by our standards, unless the family seeks help from outside. Some youngsters will defend its privacy with intense loyalty and we should respect them for this, although they may need counselling support from us in private.

Counselling is bound, in its very nature, to reveal on a greater scale than hitherto serious domestic problems to a counsellor, as his relationships with particular clients develop. Teachers who are unfamiliar with, and untrained for, the counselling role will not find these disclosures easy to accept without wanting to take some action in a desire to be helpful. Their wisest course is to tell no one and do nothing in the great majority of cases. There are, however, some heads of schools who hold the view that all information given by a client to a counsellor in schools is given within the legal framework of the educational system and that the counsellor concerned is in duty bound to pass it on to his supervisors whether the client wishes this or not. A related view is that it is very irresponsible for a teacher to enter into a confidential relationship with a client without first stating that he reserves the right to take whatever action he, the teacher, thinks is appropriate, whether the client is agreeable or not. The reasons for these opinions are varied. They may include plain conceit and a wish to cling to the traditional authority of the teacher's calling. Equally they may lie in a simpler fear of the quiet unpredictable disclosures which a counselling interview may produce. They could also be due to a managerial inability to trust subordinates, even those who have been selected and trained for counselling, by delegating responsibility to them. Perhaps they are founded in prolonged experience with deprived or disturbed children, an experience which has created an almost obsessive concern with the firm direction and practical help which such children sometimes need. But conceit, fear, authority and managerial incapacity totally stifle a counsellor's activity at its start, and

'non-confidential counselling' is almost a classic paradox. All
this is quite apart from that commonsense experience which
tells us how therapeutic it is to talk to someone in confidence
about personal difficulties, an experience which is a significant
element in the Christian confessional at its best. It is also a
fact of experience that clients who need more help than they
think their counsellors can give eventually ask them for help
from someone else, or invite them to suggest it. Beyond this,
it is wise to remember that to stand upon a point of law is not
a substitute for good personal relations: on the contrary it
more often than not indicates their complete breakdown.
Furthermore, a purely legalistic objection to confidentiality
seems to me less a valid argument than a symptom of a state of
mind which refuses to face existing facts and takes refuge behind
a screen of legal formality in the hope that problems supposedly
created by counselling will not arise. In fact they are already
with us, even if we do not all admit their existence. Moreover
the difficulties in which a teacher-counsellor can be placed by
the revelation of a client's home background or behaviour
outside school may be ameliorated by *referral*. By this I mean
the reference of the problem involved to a specialist agency
which can either support and advise the teacher-counsellor or
help the client directly as long as he and his parents are agreeable. The confidentiality of family data collected by social
agencies is an example for us all to follow here.

However, it is clear that counselling in schools by teachers
may create uncertainties, and induce stresses of various sorts
if its practitioners and their superiors are sensitive people and
are not aware of their origins and causes. Strains in school
managerial structures may also arise. The uncertainties,
stresses and strains are none the less much more a function of
ignorance about counselling and symptomatic of defects in
school communication than they are due to counselling itself
or the problems allegedly implicit in the teacher-counsellor's
dual role. In any case these problems are likely to be less than
those which already exist or are beginning to appear in schools

which still use orthodox relationships and control systems. It is true of course that schools which reputedly enjoy good staff-student relationships, schools councils, counselling services and the like exhibit transient disorders which command public attention and provoke cries for the reimposition of formal disciplinary measures. Yet these welfare arrangements and co-operative schemes inside schools are not perfect vaccines against each and every social malady which can afflict a school community. They have continually to be examined and modified when we are dealing with considerable numbers of human beings many of them at a highly volatile stage in life. Exaggerating school disturbances does not constitute a valid rebuttal of the merits of counselling and cognate activities.

When all is said and done, however, a number of excellent teachers who deal with children aged fourteen and over are sympathetic to and interested in the counselling idea. Their own relations with students often approach those of the counsellor with his client. Yet they are conditioned by their own education, professional training and experience to contemplate with some alarm the risks inherent in abandoning their traditional autocratic role as completely as the counsellor's work demands. This role may be a last defence for them in times of school unrest. Thus it is not enough for advocates of a counselling approach simply to state that the doubts of worthy professional colleagues are unfounded, or that the difficulties of counselling are illusory. For these are real enough in the sense that they exist in the minds of the teacher concerned, and while the enthusiasm of counsellors may be infectious it does not relieve them of a duty to justify their approach and to argue the doubts in commonsense terms based upon practical experience and rational thought.

Teachers do express concern about possible effects upon public classroom control which they feel might be a consequence of counselling individuals or small groups in private. Headmasters, too, are worried about loss of school discipline and the further complication of their managerial difficulties which counselling might entail. In parenthesis, we should remind ourselves that the reactions of pupils have also to be considered; for they are concerned about the good faith of this new brand of teacher who offers himself for this new service of counselling. They certainly will not be stampeded into immediate and enthusiastic acceptance of the offer, casting all their doubts and suspicions out of the classroom window simply because it is transferred into a counselling room. Counselling teachers must know what support is available, inside and outside the school when they find themselves, in the privacy of counselling, the recipients of information about clients which is serious or grave by any standards. They should know where to find such support, and they need training, *inter alia*, in judging when to use it. If they lack this essential equipment for the task of counselling they are bound to feel lonely, concerned and uncertain. Teachers who counsel are also entitled to know that the overall management decisions, taken in the school, permit, encourage and facilitate their work, as well as giving them professional protection in the unpredictable situations of the counselling relationship. A number of teachers who are interested in counselling have expressed considerable concern about the last point, with great sincerity and not as an excuse for not involving themselves in counselling.

The existence of these very real and justified anxieties has to be accepted as a starting point in any discussion of the relationship between counselling and authority and outside agencies, even if the anxieties are based on ignorance which is a result of lack of experience and guidance. But are lack of experience and uncertainty about their position the only reasons for the existence of the anxieties? We have, I suggest, to look more deeply into the teacher's role and attitude, seeking perhaps more fundamental reasons for the existence of such worries. Why do they feel the way they do about abandoning their traditional authority voluntarily? Why, also, do students have deep-rooted suspicions of teachers, the existence of which makes the teacher-counsellor's role more problematical?

The relationship between counselling and authority is further complicated by the likely possibility that those teachers who undertake a counselling role will be staff members of some experience who hold senior positions of responsibility, and that in these positions they will be expected to support by traditional methods junior colleagues who are in difficulty in classroom relations with pupils. This situation will apply especially to heads and their deputies, and to house and year masters whose special duties are part of their terms of service. If they counsel they will have a triple role to play, not just a double one; they may sometimes think it desirable to be able to counsel their colleagues as well as students. Here, too, the managerial and communication problem appears.

In general the counselling approach seems to be most useful with students in the age range of fourteen to nineteen, those who are passing through adolescence, a time of anxiety and disturbance, as it is often termed. In parenthesis, it seems that every age has its anxieties and disturbances, but the pubescent years are probably those during which the greatest help can be derived from the friendly and imperturbable ear of a counsellor. It is in this group too that the majority of school control problems seem to occur, whether or not the school population contains a sizable proportion of so-called tough, anti-social or near delinquent students, emanating from disturbed and deprived home backgrounds. These in particular might be expected to exploit the counselling situation in order to undermine the control organization of their school's teachers.

Administrators and laymen associated with the education service as well as others concerned with the much publicized aberrations of a minority of young people, are increasingly dubious or suspicious of a 'soft' or permissive approach to this tough or violent element in school populations. The general public would generally share this view. Counselling, however, is not a 'soft' approach; the contention that it is is largely based upon ignorance about its aims and methods, and upon the truth that it is not a punitive approach to personal problems, or behavioural difficulties. It is enquiring, analytical and caring. Teachers often lay emphasis in discussion on the importance of restricting counselling to those who are tough, inadequate, deprived or disturbed. Such an emphasis suggests an undue preoccupation, even a morbid one, with the unusual or abnormal student, for counselling is an approach which is relevant to the needs of all students, whatever their background, behaviour or intellectual ability. Indeed some of our students from the most stable homes, or who are intellectually most able, seem often to be in an almost desperate need of the conciliatory personal and concerned approach of a counsellor. This need can often be met without recourse to the deep treatment of the professional therapist. It does, however, demand that the counsellor abandon his concern about examination results, school uniform, his own status and the other impedimenta of school authority, and meet his client face to face as another person who is interested.

The need is there. It may indeed be a passing phase, because the special conditions of modern turbulent society and its accelerating rate of change intensify the significance of stable human relationships, or at least make mandatory the existence of people with whom such relationships can be made if the occasion demands. On the other hand the need may point the way towards new patterns in our educational system, as curriculum and other developments point towards them. In this case, the need may become a permanent feature of the system. Whether permanent or not, however, the need throws into the melting pot all our conventional ideas about authority, the teacher-image and the relation between schools and social service agencies of every sort. Everything has now to be re-examined carefully and in the light of experience, either to reassure the doubters or to assess what damage may ensue if we indulge in this quite revolutionary approach to the relation between students and staffs in schools, and indeed in establishments of further and higher education. Is the distinction between teaching and counselling quite as sharp as at first sight it appears to be? Is it possible to live with the stresses which the performance of two different roles produces. Is it within the personal resources of one person to teach formally, to counsel students and to support younger colleagues who are in difficulty? And what is school authority anyway? How much of it is a compost of habit, fear and arbitrary sanctions, rather than a respect for what is reasonable and rational? Does the paraphernalia of homework, dress, games and the rest really conduce to a development of responsibility for the young when the age of majority is now eighteen? To what extent should schools assume responsibility for the social welfare needs of their students? How far does this involve them in what seems to be prying into the affairs of their charges? Does every child from a disturbed home, or every deserted mother or divorced father really want to disclose information which troubles them emotionally? And if we do acquire social data of this kind, are we entitled to take over an anxious family's problems? Is this really a counsellor's function?

If we extend the discussion a little further, how far are the changes which threaten old educational habits unique to this particular service? Or are they but a symptom of a social readjustment or reorientation which threatens every facet of society, industry and commerce included? Teachers as much as any other group of people, are part of the whole of society, and they cannot expect to be exempt from the challenges and changes which afflict it. Counselling in schools exacts from its practitioners a wholesale reassessment not only of themselves, but of the whole career environment in which they operate. This can be a painful or strenuous experience, but it cannot be avoided. Why we do everything that we have done for so long has now to be reinvestigated, even the very organization of our schools. This is being done in other fields, in curriculum structure, in teaching techniques, in syllabus content, even in school building and planning. Yet the basic patterns of relationships in schools seem to have received less attention than any of these; and these we might think are perhaps more important than any of the just mentioned material matters to which much attention has been devoted, and in which much progress has been and is being made.

It is extremely difficult, certainly for a schoolmaster who is involved in the educational battle on the ground and in the front line, to conduct an objective research enquiry into the kind of questions I have already posed. It is also possible that while such a detailed enquiry were being conducted the situation would change so much that the results would be outdated. What can be done, however, is to look at situations which occur, and to recount how one feels about them, and to examine one's own anxieties. Whereas a research enquiry might produce firm answers and directions towards specific action, this more personal approach may only succeed in posing the questions a little more clearly. To pose the questions, however, is perhaps just what we must do, for my impression is that teachers, in the main, are still not looking at the right questions. Whatever these questions are, and some of them have been hinted at in this chapter, the answers cannot be imposed upon individual teachers by order or administrative instruction. This is because people cannot be compelled to counsel, because it is not the kind of activity which conscripts can perform, any more than they can be workers for the Samaritans, marriage counsellors or members of a parish council under duress. In the very nature of the job they have to be volunteers impelled by their own spontaneous concern for people. Counselling requires its practitioners to look at every possible question about school life and organization which any one of a thousand clients can and will produce in the quiet security of a counselling interview. And as soon as the client asks any question he puts at risk the view which his counsellor has about the question which his client presents. As we shall see in later pages, once a counsellor is committed he cannot withdraw without damaging not only himself but also, and more important, his client, and the latter's views of the counsellor's generation and society.

To begin with we can now go on to look at counselling itself somewhat briefly, and from that point examine the implications in day-to-day terms which it carries for other more long-standing school activities and practices.

Aspects of counselling

1 *Counselling*

Counselling is basically a psychological process as a result of which a person's personality and behaviour may be modified and improved, in the everyday commonsense meanings of these words. Teachers might be expected to welcome warmly the use of 'improvement' and seize avidly the possibilities which counselling thus appears to offer for ensuring conformity with school regimes. They should, however, pause to think whether such conformity DOES OR CAN lead to a significant long-term improvement or modification of a student's personality and character, as distinct from short-term compliance with an arbitrary set of school or college rules. We must be quite unequivocal about the principle that counselling is directed to the personal needs of the individual client in front of his counsellor, not to buttressing the sometimes shaky edifice of school regulations or supporting the self-esteem of a school staff.

To return to the improvement or modification, however, this comes about because counselling helps the client to learn new ways of understanding himself and his feelings, and of responding to his own ideas and emotions: and not only of understanding and responding to himself, but also the physical world around him and the social environment in which he lives and moves. This kind of learning requires for its fulfilment a personal relationship between the client and his counsellor which the former values. Why he values it is not at this stage important, although it is sometimes useful to explore this at some point in counselling. Whether the client consciously realizes it or not, however, the relationship provides him with security which, at the particular point in his life or development when he has benefit of counselling, may be the only real security he knows. For him, this may be something really dependable at a moment of great doubt and uncertainty. Within the framework of this relationship, anything that the client says about his situation and feelings, and the discussion of what he says are components of the whole therapeutic process of counselling. We should emphasize here that the counsellor's attention is focused not only on what the client says about his circumstances, but also takes into account how he feels about the circumstances he describes, even if these feelings appear to be quite unjustified or irrational in the mind of a detached and uninvolved observer.

The client's feelings are important because among other things they affect his ability to consider advice which is pertinent but which he cannot accept; they may lead him into antisocial behaviour inside and outside school; they may be quite transient, or more persistent. In a phrase, they are important because they influence what he is doing or may do in the future. He may be fully aware of them, or he may not. In either case, the counsellor has to take them into serious consideration; he must start with them as a fact of the client's life. If he does not accept them he is really telling the client that he is an idiot to start with. This is not helpful, although it may turn out during counselling that the client comes to realize this himself. If this is so the client has at least begun to understand himself a little better than he did at the beginning of the process, but it is never the counsellor's purpose to tell him this, or lead him to such a conclusion.

Thus the client is helped by his counsellor to learn more about himself, not about English or mathematics or whatever else he has to learn in the formal school sense, but about himself as a person. This process is therapeutic because it can lead to mitigation or cure of the anxieties and disturbances with which he is assailed or feels himself to be assailed. It can only be effective when it is wholly private to both client and counsellor unless both agree otherwise. Other facets of the counsellor's role will emerge in later sections of this chapter.

2 Teaching and counselling

Teaching and counselling seem to have some common ground in the encouragement of a drive to learn. But the resemblance between counselling and teaching seems to end almost as soon as it has begun: for teachers' actions are or have usually been directed to intellectual learning through talking, demonstrating and instructing about events, things and other people, all outside the student's own life and individuality so that his personality and emotions are neglected. The orthodox teaching process is not primarily concerned with these last two matters. Moreover traditional teaching drives information and knowledge into the student, whereas the counsellor elicits experiences and feelings from his client. Yet this antithesis between the approach of traditional teaching and counselling is not quite so complete as it might seem to be on first examination. Sensitive teachers, skilled in the craft and art which are essential components of their occupation, will realize that while their methods are generally directed to plain indoctrination of one kind or another, sometimes at least they have to draw something out of their students. After all, this is what education in the broadest sense is about. Teachers of this quality will understand too the possibility or reality of a positive correlation between enjoying their formal teaching and understanding the experience and feelings of the students they teach. They will also realize that success in the former may depend upon the degree to which their students understand themselves and are free from psychological stress. Furthermore, such teachers will understand that this in turn is dependent upon the quality

c

of the relationship between them and their students. So it is with counselling: the nature and meaning of the client-counsellor relationship is the basis of the distinction between orthodox teaching and counselling.

3 The client-counsellor relationship

This relationship must be one of partnership based upon mutual respect and equality as human beings, regardless of age. Only on this basis can counsellor and client work together in harmony and mutual confidence towards a solution of any problems which the client presents, or understanding and handling any situation in which he finds himself. The words 'solution' and 'handling' may suggest that the counsellor must take positive action on the client's behalf. The nature of counselling largely precludes such a course, for the counsellor's role in the relationship with his clients is to help the latter to reach their own decisions about future action where this is appropriate, or to live with a situation about which nothing can be done, at least for the present. The counsellor's task in plain terms is to help a client to help himself, not to tell him what to do. It is important to understand at this point that a stage may be reached in the relationship at which the client asks for advice because he is ready to consider and indeed to accept it; but it is not the counsellor's task to give this at the outset, nor is it the purpose of counselling. Once it has been invited, however, it seems to me that counsellors dealing with young people should not shirk the duty or responsibility of giving it, although the onus of accepting or rejecting it still lies with the young client.

To encourage the client to help himself requires of the counsellor something more than the mere abandonment of imposed authority on his part. This is a purely negative attribute, although none the less essential. He needs also care, patience and an infinite capacity for listening, as well as the insight and skill to evoke, by appropriate comment or question,

the client's explanation or evaluation, even in the simplest
and most halting terms, of his troubles and situation. He does
not need the capacity to manage and take over other people's
lives for them. This may be left to different people. A relationship must be made if the client is to gain the greatest benefit
from these qualities in the counsellor through which the client
trusts or 'takes to' the counsellor. The nurture of that
relationship from its tentative beginnings into one which is
significant to the client is part of the counsellor's responsibility.
This is partly dependent on what the client feels about the
counsellor and thus on the impression the latter makes. The
latter must seem to be what he is, and be what he seems to be.
It seems almost superfluous to add that there is really very
little room in counselling, be it with individuals or groups, for
the flashy extrovert or the moody introvert: the one may reek
of insincerity, the other be almost incommunicable, and neither
will find it easy to create a relationship which is significant to
the client. In counselling a group one young client once said
to me, 'You talk too much, this is not a time for the extrovertism
of schoolmasters'; on another I was told that I was too gloomy
to be helpful, and yet again that people who write about
counselling should not lose their tempers. I use these illustrations simply to emphasize the irritation which may be caused
even by transient moods, to which all of us are subject at one
time or another to varying degrees. Each of them was a fair
comment upon my handling of a particular counselling situation
at a certain stage in its development. Each exemplifies the client's
sensitivity to his counsellor's attitude. All three of them also
highlight the nature of the relationship between me and the
students in the group who uttered them: they felt that the
relationship was strong enough not to be broken or strained by
blunt comment of this kind. They judged it correctly, and
assumed that I had totally abandoned the formal authority
with which I as deputy head of the school was endowed.
This state of ease and relaxation with the clients concerned was
not necessarily easily and quickly reached. The first meeting

or two with the group was really a careful exploration of one another's feelings and reactions, as they moved gingerly towards a partnership with a senior schoolmaster. This was a new experience for them. As another student put it, 'Making this kind of relaxed mutually trusting relationship with a schoolmaster was like putting one's foot into the cold sea; you test it to see your reaction: you work up carefully hoping you can get used to it, and for a long time you are very quick to withdraw.' While his clients are 'getting used' to it, the counsellor has to keep cool, to encourage, to listen, to be patient, above all to accept whatever comes and be free from moody instability.

The ability to accept whatever the client says is perhaps the real test of the counsellor's relationship with his client: to accept not because what the client says is true, but because it is the inevitable starting point from which the counsellor helps the client to think about his own problem and situation: to accept, in a situation which is wholly private and confidential, unless both client and counsellor agree otherwise. We shall return to the point later, but there is a vital distinction here between the honest private candour of the client-counsellor relationship in individual or group counselling and the still fundamental conflict which pervades many teacher-pupil relationships in the public glare of the classroom. In the quiet privacy of the counselling room anything and everything can be discussed as part of helping the client to understand his situation and to act upon or live with it. Much that has rightly been called social dynamite in terms of home situations and other difficulties which a client might not like to be the public property of the staff or classroom can be disclosed in that privacy and in the secure knowledge that it will be accepted but not publicized by the counsellor. Such disclosures put to him in private may indeed subject a counsellor to considerable stress, if only because they may seem so serious to him that he cannot cope with them. It is, however, for selection and training procedures to provide counsellors who can tolerate such stress conditions and know how to deal with them. Moreover the meaning which a client attaches to the relationship with his counsellor postulates that the latter must be aware of his own limitations and not take upon himself burdens which he is personally or professionally incapable of sustaining. A failure to bear them adequately may be harmful to his client. This also emphasizes the importance of referral.

4 *What the counsellor offers*

So far so good. We ought to ask, however, what a counsellor offers to his client which a sensitive teacher does not give. Teachers, and those in other occupations which contain a large element of personal service, will properly claim that 'they give of themselves' quite apart from any specialized expertise which is the stock-in-trade of their calling. Yet apart from some special skill and knowledge, a relaxed manner, sensitivity to others, endless patience, mental lucidity, counsellors require perceptiveness. Perhaps this is a sort of intuitiveness in dealing with people which is almost indefinable, but analogous to the ability of engineers to cure the maladies of machinery without being able at the precise moment to say why they have effected the cure.

There are, of course, risks in describing the perceptiveness of a counsellor in such imprecise terms; it opens the door, almost dangerously, to the slickness of the confidence trickster and the quack. No qualities apply less to the counsellor than that. This distinguishing mark is that he is concerned about the fact that other people who are in trouble exist. He is receptive to what these people have to tell him, but not dedicated to converting them to a particular point of view or line of conduct.

Teachers with whom I have discussed it find this last phrase especially confusing. They say, and rightly, that they can often see clearly what their young charges ought to do to achieve some degree of personal serenity, peace of mind, a decent job or academic success. They have experience. They are anxious to pass this on, so that younger people may avoid the mistakes which they may have made themselves, or seen others make, and the consequences of which are potentially disastrous however we look at them. But even doctors' patients do not always accept a prescribed course of treatment; and teachers certainly know that their students do not always do the work set for them. Prescriptive guidance is no use unless the recipient is in the frame of mind to accept and act upon it certainly in this day and age. If he does not care that rejecting the offered guidance will be to his disadvantage, whatever that guidance is, then it can be no use to him. Many of my clients have probably considered various alternative forms of advice and rejected them in advance because they could not bring themselves to act upon them. For those who are sensitive, lucid and abounding in sagacious and valid advice it is variously disappointing, frustrating or insulting to have it rejected. It is easy to move to the next stage of regarding such rejection as downright stupid, at which point communication ceases. With the greatest possible respect to my professional colleagues all over this country, these are common reactions on the part of many of them – and not out of any ill-will to their students – but simply because they are so perspicacious about other people's affairs, and so conditioned to direct them, that they cannot understand why their advice should be disregarded.

We can expect sixteen-year-olds to reject advice from adults, simply because it comes from adults; or because their experience of adults is that they give orders and instructions often without courtesy, frequently with vehemence and sometimes with violence. We live in a world confused by the fact of breakdown in communication between the generations for these and other reasons which are the subject of abundant comment and query all the time. The reasons are important enough for understanding the facts; but for a counsellor the facts of loss of contact between generations, and increasing independence of young people are those to which he reacts by offering himself simply as a person. Thus a counsellor presents himself first of all as another human being, accepting his client and acceptable to him, who does not wish to impose himself or his ideas upon his clients. It is perfectly true that a limited number of teachers do just this and have done for some time simply because they are sensitive, serene, at peace with themselves and have totally discarded their authoritarian trappings. As counsellors do, they say in effect to their students, 'You can make a relationship with me in which we trust one another as far as any human beings can. Once we have done this we can look together in private at the problem that troubles you.' A young client who is suspicious of adults, and who can understand this offer, is then able to relax because the counsellor cares about him as he is, not as he might wish him to be, for no other reason than the fact of his existence as another human being. Certainly a client may realize in due time the value of his counsellor's experience and knowledge, and whatever other qualities are part of him: but the counsellor presents himself as a person first of all. This it is which helps him to reach a stage wherein he can seek advice seriously and enhance his sense of responsibilities for his own affairs.

People need other people, and counsellors probably meet this fundamental human need; they meet it effectively because they have no self interest to advance, and no emotional entanglements to inhibit a calm joint appraisal of the client's needs. Clearly such an attitude on the part of the counsellor does not threaten the client in any way: the latter is not presented with a 'do this or else' situation, and he does not need to react defensively to his counsellor.

As we have already seen, young clients may at first react in precisely this manner because they expect some kind of dogmatic approach from an adult. Even so, they abandon this defensive, even resentful reaction as soon as they realize that it does not upset the counsellor, that the latter is not injecting into the relationship his own scale of values nor imposing solutions for the client's problems, and that his contribution as a person to the relationship is simply to help the client improve his own position by his own thinking and his own efforts. The client recognizes the quality of the counsellor and of the relationship he offers. He therefore realizes that defensive and self-deceiving reactions on his part are irrelevant and pointless. Consequently he sees that he runs no risk at all from complete honesty and candour within the security which the relationship offers.

Given all this, however, what is the distinction, if any, between counsellors as I see them, and kindly, sensitive teachers? This is the $64,000 question, to which I believe there are two perfectly clear answers. First, no matter how kindly and humane a teacher is, he cannot be the counsellor if he consciously holds in reserve *to any degree*, however small, the imposition on his students of the authority which goes with his position. That species of authority is markedly different from the authority which is attributed to him because he is the sort of person he seems to be to his students. The latter is moral authority not needing the threat of sanctions; the former is hierarchical authority sustained by the threat of sanctions. We shall discuss this further in the succeeding chapter.

The second part of the answer is that a counsellor has to be prepared to recognize his own inadequacy, to himself and to his clients if necessary. This is difficult enough for most of us to do in all conscience, and especially so for teachers who often assume that to recognize their own inadequacy is the same as losing control, or admitting defeat in an emotional sense. Control and defeat are not in the counsellor's vocabulary. He does not control his clients; he works with them. They do not defeat him; they simply no longer require his services or need more skilled service than he can give.

The point is perhaps illustrated by a drawn-out series of counselling sessions with a moderately intelligent group of six seventeen-year-olds. They were certainly not 'high-flyers' but they had some potential for advanced-level study, conditioned by an ability to challenge anything and everything within and without the school. They approached me about holding a series of counselling meetings out of school hours, in the belief that this might help them to 'unravel themselves' as one of them put it, and to realize their potential without 'going mad' in the process. We began well enough, and the group developed a cohesive relationship which showed itself able to tolerate much very frank discussion and self-examination. We met once a week for about twelve weeks. During the last three or four sessions I began to feel quite anxious and inadequate: the group seemed to me to have lost any sense of purpose or direction, and one or two of them began to hint at this most politely as I realized afterwards. At what turned out to be the final session I expressed my feelings to them and invited their comment. Two of them said, 'You have lost your earlier "sharpness".' They openly admitted that there seemed no longer any point in continuing the meetings. Although from time to time one or two of them came to me individually, the group as such never met again. Perhaps it had run its useful course. Perhaps the contemporaneous absence of my chief subject colleague induced a weariness which made it impossible for me to see the possible further development of the group. Possibly I could, in any case, no longer tolerate the considerable and unique stresses which this particular group imposed on me, stresses which the group itself freely recognized. It may even be that to wind up the meetings was the most useful thing I did with it, because I showed it was possible to recognize and admit my own incapacity to a group of young adults, without losing contact with them.

All this means that there is something more to counselling than being kind and sensitive, or commanding respect by being the sort of person one is. In summary this something more is a total abandonment of any formal authority plus an ability to recognize one's own frailties in a wide variety of unforeseen circumstances. Perhaps there is a subtlety about these additional qualities which puts them beyond complete understanding.

On the other hand, those who believe this may be implying that they are themselves unsuitable for counselling.

5 *The depth of school counselling*

In terms of psychological theory this kind of counselling has some likeness to the Rogerian school of client-centred therapy initiated by the American psychologist, Carl Rogers. He and his followers lay great stress upon the capacity within every human being for self-development towards personal harmony and self-responsibility. Rogerian counsellors emphasize the clinical value derivable from a client's completely frank expression of his thoughts and feelings. Such counsellors make little or no attempt to interpret or evaluate what their clients say. The latter are allowed to follow whatever lines of thought occur to them, so as to clarify their ideas and emotions. The counsellors do not focus their client's attention upon past experiences and feelings which they, the counsellors, may rightly or wrongly think are specially significant. In simpler terms, Rogerian counselling may be looked upon as a way of 'talking out' the problems, situations and feelings which the client believes himself to be assailed with. There is, of course, a built-in assumption here, which is not always justified, that the client has the experience, articulateness and control to express himself lucidly. Lucidity and experience are, however, vital parts of the counsellor's contribution to the discussion. He provides what the client cannot provide. His clarity of expression and perceptiveness of thought come to the client's aid when he is halting and confused. His demeanour prompts a reserved or resentful client into discussing his situation. The relationship between client and counsellor provides the milieu in which the discussion is possible, and it is the counsellor's task to initiate it.

Of course, teacher-counsellors should not expect to achieve the depth of counselling of which a professional Rogerian therapist is capable. The general likeness remains however, and there are interesting parallels to be found in the views of Carl Jung about the significance in psychotherapy of the relationship between counsellor and client.*

'I have no ready-made philosophy to hand out when a patient asks me, "What do you advise?" "What shall I do?" I do not know any better than he. I know only one thing; that when to my conscious outlook there is no possible way of going ahead, and I am therefore "stuck", my unconscious will react to the unbearable standstill.' The point which Jung makes is that the outcome of the meeting between patient and analyst is uncertain. He goes on, 'We cannot by any device bring it about that the treatment is not the outcome of a mutual influence in which the whole being of the patient as well as that of the doctor plays its part.' If for patient, we read client, for doctor counsellor, and for mutual influence relationship, this assertion remains generally valid. Jung laid great emphasis on the demands which the all-important relationship makes upon the counsellor's personality, his frankness about himself, his willingness to change, his patience and perseverance. He further writes that under these conditions 'psychotherapy ceases to be a mere method for treating the sick. It is now of service to the healthy as well, at least to those who have a right to psychic health, and whose illness is the suffering that tortures us all.' And so is counselling by teachers in their schools, for, in the broadest sense it is psychotherapeutic.

When all is said and done, however, discussion of counselling in schools is still somewhat vitiated by the persistent belief that such a process is solely a matter for highly trained and skilled experts in the behavioural sciences; clinical psychologists, psychotherapists, psychoanalysts and psychiatrists, who are variously competent in coping with clients' behaviour problems and able to recognize and treat mental disorder and disease. Who then are teachers to interfere in this specialized field of human adjustment and maladjustment which required long and special training? On the other hand, we might also

* See No. I in 'Suggestions for further reading'.

ask which group of public servants is better placed to work in the field of adolescent behaviour? After all children are by law under teachers' care and influence for at least ten years. The answer to these questions lies in the title of this section, 'the depth of school counselling'. By this I mean the degree of sophistication and complexity of treatment – and counselling by teachers in schools is after all a form of treatment. Explanatory analogies are often dangerous but there is a simple parallel in everyday life: taking a couple of aspirins for a headache is a shallow and unsophisticated treatment, whereas the use of advanced drugs for the treatment of schizophrenia is a deep and complex matter requiring skilled supervision. Moreover, if the simple medication either does not effect an immediate cure, or needs to be repeated at regular intervals to maintain an apparent cure, then this is an indication that a more serious condition may exist, which demands more elaborate examination and more sophisticated treatment. I am not saying that counselling by teachers is as elementary and superficial as taking an aspirin: equally it is not so profound as advanced drug therapy.

I am saying two things, therefore: that the *relative* shallowness of counselling by teachers could conceivably prevent the development of a simple situation into a serious social and mental problem; and secondly that if it seems to be an interminable need of the client, if he comes to regard the counsellor as an essential and continuous prop, or if it exposes in other ways the possibility of certain behaviour or personality syndromes, then more expert help or advice is needed than the teacher-counsellor can give. Such a case must be dealt with by referral. Training for teachers who wish to counsel must therefore include some discussion and recognition of symptoms of personality and behaviour disorder, as well as an understanding of their own limitations.

Such a form of 'middle-depth' counselling by teachers is, in the clinical sense, a form of preventive social medicine, if for no other reason than that the trusting relationship between counsellor and client often seems to be therapeutic in itself, because it gives to the client a sense of value and individuality – or he believes that it does. This belief is important to him. This may, of course, be a rather unscientific and subjective view, as ideas about relationships often are, but in practice it seems sometimes at least to make very good sense in terms of the results that follow in a school. As a teaching colleague of mine said some years ago, 'If the relationships are right within a school, the work, the conduct, the sense of responsibility among the students follow almost automatically.' There are schools in which there is a strained atmosphere which can be felt almost as soon as one enters the main door; in which there are bad relationships among the staff, and abundant trouble between staff and students to maintain control and work standards. Equally there are others in which there is no stress or trouble, because, as my colleague observed, the relationships within the school are right. Counselling is at least one step beyond this rather vague assumption of good relationships; it is a slightly more personal means towards establishing, as a deliberate act of policy rather than just letting them happen, the harmonious relationships and peace of mind which can thus prevent the personal stress and social disturbance which exists in too many schools and other institutions of education. Behind it lie the resources of social agencies, medical services and psychological guidance if they are needed. There is no need for such counselling in school to be clinically deep, as if we were always dealing with disturbed psychopaths. And some workers in the youth field, especially those involved in operations detached from specific youth organizations, will pay tribute to the value of relations at a personal but not analytical level, which can influence lost and lonely adolescents on the fringe of, if not actually concerned in, delinquent activities in the depressing deserts of our larger towns and cities. These workers are not specialized analysts of behaviour, but human beings, who with skill, patience, concern and courage accept and value people as they find them. This is the teacher-counsellor's role within his school, for which he must have continuous in-service training and follow-up support.

6 *Counselling and pastoral care*

Counselling is one of the most ill-used words in education today. Teachers and other educationalists appear at times to use it to describe every kind of informal school activity involving teachers and students, with the possible exception of physical, dramatic and musical pursuits. Many teachers with whom I have discussed the subject during the past few years have assumed that counselling includes avuncular chats of the 'don't do it again, lad' type, answers to enquiries about future careers, relaxed informal discussions about current events, social welfare in the sense of material provision for deprived children, home-visiting and customary gentle but firm surveillance of work and conduct. They have said that there is no need to conjure up the word 'counselling' to describe these ordinarily acceptable kinds of pastoral care in school with which they have long been familiar. These teaching colleagues have not understood, however, that none of these thoroughly desirable and useful activities necessarily carries any hint of a real relationship between them and their students, or, as I would put it, between counsellor and client; the traditional authoritarian position of the teacher is never totally abandoned. The implications of a real partnership between client and counsellor on terms of equality between individuals are not understood. Yet teachers have claimed that they 'do counselling' simply because they involve themselves, certainly with complete goodwill, in these vaguely paternalistic activities. They assume the title if not the status of counsellor without seriously understanding what counselling really means. This, however, is without prejudice to their professional teaching competence.

There is thus a continuing confusion in the minds of teachers about counselling, and among administrators, laymen who have educational responsibilities, as well as parents. On reflection it really should be clear that the word 'counselling' cannot be applied to two radically different activities: on the one hand busily doing things for other people or telling them what to do on the assumption that they want them done; and on the other, making a private, serene and therapeutic relationship between counsellor and client in which the latter learns how to do things for himself. The first is a dependent relationship; the second is not. Avuncular chats may have a temporarily soothing effect on students, social welfare may provide material needs; but neither is specifically directed, as counselling is, to the needs of the client's personality and character. Moreover, in the sense that general pastoral care may enhance one person's dependence upon another it may actually impede the growth of his character and sense of responsibility which counselling is intended to foster. In very simple terms the difference between pastoral care and counselling is that between 'What can I do for you?' and 'What can you do for yourself?' These comments apply with equal force whether the counsellor is dealing with an individual or a group of individuals. Although the group situation may be more intricate and taxing in some respects, the counsellor's aims, qualities and attitudes are the same. To deal with the complexities of group counselling in this volume would obscure its central purpose.

7 Counselling and other agencies

The distinction which has to be made between counselling and social welfare is one which depends for clarification upon a full understanding of the acceptance, personal-relational and non-authoritarian basis of counselling and its complete freedom from any sort of take-over implications as far as the client's life is concerned. The distinction is, I think, assisted by looking at two possible relations between counselling and social welfare services. In the first place personal counselling can be used parallel with or alongside a variety of statutory social agencies: among these I would include the Youth Employment

Service, Probation Officers, the Police Liaison Scheme where this exists, School Medical Services and the Education Welfare Service, each of which has a defined role in society. All of these may be involved in helping or correcting a student while he is at school and experiencing counselling; the latter helps him to develop his own sense of responsibility while another agency is operating in a different and more directive field. I appreciate that this has to be done in concert between the counsellor and the other agency's personnel, and I return to this in referral. The vital point here is that counselling in school does not replace the valuable work of these other services, still less the work of home-visiting teachers, or careers staff. It simply gives the client personal support at a time of difficulty. It is doing a different job, in its own right.

In the second place, counselling can usefully be the precursor of help by such agencies, or the medium through which they may be involved in helping positively a client or his family. Adolescents are often very independent and proud, and resent at first the prospect of some outside body interfering in their own or their family's lives, because they feel that it degrades their self-respect: they may equally be suspicious rather than independent, for help may be regarded as interference and intrusion. Counselling can be helpful in dispelling suspicion and resentment, without detracting from independence, pride and self-respect, so that aid provided by an outside agency is understood in advance and appreciated afterwards. In the chapter on referral more attention is paid to the ways in which outside organizations and counselling may work together.

8 *The purpose of counselling*

The effect upon school order and control with which this book is partly concerned must be a function of the purpose of counselling. Without dwelling at undue length upon this we ought to be as clear as possible about it, although its outcome in particular cases is uncertain. The kind of individual or group counselling with which I am concerned is intended to increase a client's sense of responsibility for his own life, to help him to make up his own mind and to act upon his decisions; to cope sensibly with situations he has hitherto disliked, resented or rejected: and to come to terms with circumstances which cannot for the moment be changed. It is not a soft process, indeed it is often a severely taxing experience, in which the counsellor's concern and interest may be the means by which the young client is nursed through a period of uncertainty and irresponsibility. We cannot define the purpose of counselling in more concrete terms than these. In the specifically school situation it is important to understand, however, that one of the aims might well be to help a client at the very least to tolerate teachers with whom he is in constant trouble, and not to add to the difficulties of his own situation by continuous disturbances. In short the counselling is intended to improve relationships within the school, not to undermine the influence of the counsellor's teaching colleagues even if this means, as it sometimes must, that the client must show more sense than the adult teacher! Thus the enhancement of client responsibility is a means to an end which itself benefits the whole school.

9 *Voluntary nature of counselling*

It needs emphasis that a counselling service in a school does not mean that every student in that school has to be counselled, whether he likes it or not. There are probably enough intruders into the privacy of personal life without the addition of another intrusive agency to the list. Counselling is a service which is there if it is needed. It is not to be imposed. On the other hand, if a client wants to discuss with his counsellor in school problems of his home life he must feel at liberty to do so in the knowledge that what he says will be treated with confidence and not become the current gossip topic of the staff-room. In some cases there is no doubt student-parent relationships are improved by

D

the use of purely student counselling. The relationship between this and home visiting will be dealt with later under referral. There is however no compulsion upon a student to disclose what if anything is wrong at home, and my impression is that urgent if well-meaning attempts to pry into home background can create resentment which only exacerbates the client's feelings about himself and his school anyway, so that the final situation is worse than the first. This is scarcely the aim of counselling. We need, I think, to remember that the majority of young people are very healthy in every respect and will grow up in this way without undue interference from outside bodies. We should not look for troubles that are not there, or assume that everyone has problems with which they cannot cope. We may well create problems if we do. Of course we may at times be resentful that problems of which we feel we ought to have knowledge ourselves are revealed independently by outside agencies, but this is not a justification for prying into the affairs of people who may well prefer to leave them in the hands of people outside the school because they may suspect the latter's motives. In essence, counsellors exist because they are needed, not to create work for themselves in the image of the do-gooder or to enhance their own self-esteem.

There is, however, a case to be made for inviting certain students to counselling for special reasons because it may be obvious that they will never bring themselves to the counsellor's door.

The difficulties associated with such staff-initiated counselling were discussed in my earlier book, and I do not wish to repeat them here. Two conditions must be satisfied, however. The first is that it should only be initiated after very sober discussion with the counsellor of an intended and unwitting client's case, as far as it is known, by the staff who teach him, and in a desire to help his personal development rather than to correct him in the sense of ensuring his conformity. The second follows from the first and is that the counsellor must not become the refuse-dump for every student who has trouble with an individual teacher. This vitiates his purpose. He is not a last-ditch defence for erring or incompetent or inexperienced teachers. Any abandonment of the essentially voluntary nature of counselling must therefore be fraught with the utmost caution, and consideration of each individual case.

This outline of counselling may seem to the orthodox or merely cynical teacher to amount only to so much theoretical verbiage. It is not easy to describe the counselling process and what it entails in exact or objective terms. It is perhaps a workable way of dealing with adults, but scarcely some believe for adolescents, volatile, lacking in knowledge, experience and wisdom. They ought, it might be said, to defer to age anyway, assuming that age is necessarily worth deferring to. Yet if the counsellor's qualities as a person and the counsellor-client relationship are sufficiently meritorious, the young client may come to think that the particular sample of age (represented by his counsellor) is worth communicating with, without deferring to. For the person and the relationship matter above all, and are the determining factors in making a joint solution of a given problem or situation feasible. The relationship I have dealt with. In what lies the quality of the counsellor? Insight, patience, understanding, self-awareness I have already catalogued. To them we must add stability, serenity, imperturbability, even unshockability. The qualities of a saint? Perhaps. But there are saints in these terms in the teaching profession and some, if not many, who might reveal these qualities if given the opportunities and support for displaying them. By support, I mean a school managerial structure and social ethos which recognize that the caring activities of counsellors are relevant and helpful to the conduct of the whole school, as well as to the needs of individual students. To these matters we can now direct our attention.

III

The conflicting roles

In its bare essentials the concept of conflicting roles is that teaching and counselling are different activities; that they are so different as to be antithetic; that, therefore, any teacher who attempts both activities in his own school must experience considerable conflicts in his mind; and that these conflicts may be of such a magnitude as to be intolerable and in any case will prevent him performing either duty satisfactorily.

We shall see shortly whether the basic premise, i.e. that the two activities are antithetic, is universally valid. For the moment let us consider the general social and philosophical environment in which we are discussing whether the roles of counsellor and teacher are antagonistic. To begin with, experience of counselling in Britain is still very limited, and the practice of it is spreading but slowly. Objective research is therefore also limited. Moreover research is itself not easy to conduct, because counselling involves personal attitudes and interpersonal relationships. Rigorous investigation into these and cognate topics are intrinsically difficult because of their obvious complexity. This complexity is rooted in the fact that attitudes of and relationships between people are parts of an interwoven network of reactions and counter-reactions. Beside this intricate situation, the physical scientist's study of interactions between the most complex non-living substances are mere child's play. For many educationalists, therefore, counselling itself is not only a purely theoretical concept for them in the sense that they have no practical experience upon which they could base a judgement about its feasibility; it is also a subject about which valid evidence and hard information is scarce, pragmatic experience apart. While we should not discount the limited research and comment which is available, views about the conflict of roles tend to be based upon subjective feelings and opinions, and the expectation of teachers' reactions to an approach to their job with which, in the nature of the present situation, they cannot be familiar. Moreover they cannot easily visualize or read about any situation, an evaluation of which cannot be easily carried out. This is clearly a difficult circumstance in which to make a sensible judgement.

At this point we are introducing a general human attitude which is not limited specially to educationalists' views about counselling. To think about counselling and its implications for a teacher postulates considering a major change in the relationships which teachers make with their students. In the absence of practical experience and an extensive literature, this postulate in turn demands an imaginative extrapolation from the known familiar relationships of the conventional teacher into the unfamiliar or hard-to-imagine relationships of counselling. Any kind of extrapolation, from the commonplace experience of present everyday life towards methods and events which have yet to be experienced, strains the capacity of most people. An illustration may help here. If we think back for a moment, a man in the year 1900 might well have found it difficult to imagine that he or his immediate offspring would ever be able to sit in his own house and watch a football match being played six thousand miles away. The current space odysseys of the TV programme 'Startrek' are derided by a lot of people, who forget the extent to which the imaginative prognostications of H. G. Wells and Jules Verne have become today's commonplace, despite the sheer incredulity with which they were regarded when they were first written. In any event, practical accomplishment vindicates visionaries and converts the sceptics. The history of educational practice contributes to this generalization, as advocates of new methods and attitudes have experienced all too often. Without being unfair to them, teachers are no exception to a quite widespread human inability to visualize revolutionary change or great leaps forward in social action and achievement. It may, of course, be that they cannot conceive that in the specific field of teaching and counselling the personal relationships of their work should be radically different from those with which they are conversant: it may also be the case that they can conceive of such possibilities but recoil from them because they feel that they could not cope, emotionally or otherwise, with the unpredictable situations which such new relationships might bring in their train. Which of these reasons is the correct one does not matter here: in any case it is likely to be one for one person and another for another. What does matter is that this general human attitude and the causes of it are part of any teacher's make-up. This is a vitally important part of the argument about the conflict of roles, an argument which really cannot be properly resolved until those who make a judgement about it have an imaginative understanding of what counselling really is about. Here is the real dilemma, for if the exploration of man's external environment of the world and space presents difficulties to quite intelligent people, it is scarcely surprising that the internal environment of man's feelings and relationships presents greater problems of visualization to those who do not as yet explore it by counselling or indeed by the more specialized methods of psychotherapy and clinical psychology. For the teacher who essays this kind of exploration in his own school, wherein he is himself part of the environment in which he is helping his clients to live, it is a matter of even greater intricacy. We should not risk deceiving ourselves that it is not. None the less, the existence of difficulties is no excuse for not trying to overcome them. To indulge in this particular form of escapism is to deny progress and improvement in the work we do.

We must be fair here, however. Few educators of any rank will deny that some very significant and exciting changes in educational practice have taken place within recent years albeit not without much initial scepticism. This is especially true of school building, curriculum content, subject matter, classroom materials and instructional techniques. The successful influence of the Schools' Council's and the Nuffield Foundation's various projects are valid evidence of the readiness of teachers to innovate when they are properly prepared for doing so by the provision of valid evidence, clear information and adequate guidance. These three give teachers a sound foundation, based upon the experience and experimentation of others, on which they can build their individual edifices of innovation and experiment. In parenthesis, however, it is worth noting here that some teachers regard the literature of these projects as bibles to be followed to the letter – a new form of educational fundamentalism which permits no individual heresies – instead of guides through uncharted country in which the teacher concerned must use his own judgement to some extent at least. Be this as it may, new techniques can be demonstrated, materials displayed, course contents published, and curricular plans shown. All who are interested can thus see, study and consider them. Changes in relationships between people are however much more difficult to project into the comprehension of man. Such changes are not concrete entities which can be seen, handled and heard, and their possible outcomes predicted with some degree of accuracy. All is uncertain to very uncertain beholders. When we talk about the methods and effects of the counsellor's activities upon his clients and especially upon himself, we are talking about the intricate interactions between the personality characteristics and personal philosophy of one person and those of another. Even for those who welcome change eagerly, uncertainty about the outcome of such complex reactions as those of the counselling situation is infinitely greater than that associable with the introduction of a new instructional technique.

The concept of conflicting roles thus owes its existence at least in part to fears which have their roots in this uncertainty and the risks which consequently must seem to be associated with it.

It will be helpful to remind ourselves at this point, perhaps by way of reassurance that fears of new relationships are not confined to those who work in education. Discussion with friends outside teaching suggests that industrial and business management is confronted by similar problems and uncertainties. If relationships in these areas of human activity are breaking down – as they are to some extent in education – what patterns of relationship should replace them? To what extent should those whose job it is to carry responsibility and make decisions treat those in their employment who make or do things as equal partners in a common enterprise? Does such a theory of partnership entail simply that management accords to the man on the factory-floor or the girl in the typing-pool a dignity and respect which stem solely from their existence as human beings? Or does such a theory mean that these people have to be consulted about every decision which management has to make? Does a manager's or director's authority over his subordinates derive merely from the status of the position he occupies or does it owe its effectiveness to his being the sort of person his subordinates think he is? Questions of this kind are those which heads of schools, and their employers, as well as senior colleagues, have also to answer especially when they consider counselling services. There is some evidence in these other fields of human relationships that the personal quality of the man who carries responsibility matters at least as much as the position he occupies or his professional qualifications. Upon this rather nebulous quality may depend the extent to which the decisions he has to make, because his is a decision-making position, will be acceptable and actionable by those who are below him in the organizational hierarchy. If this is true, his personal qualities, including open-mindedness and approachability, far from undermining his positional authority. will actually support it. We shall look at this more fully in Chapter IV.

We cannot remind ourselves too often or too forcibly that counselling is about human relationships, not about a mechanical and precise technique. Human relationships in every branch of our society's activities are in a state of flux, and this fluid situation applies to the personal relations of education as much as to any other area of human action. The very fact that industrialists and business managers are being compelled to re-think their human relations only adds urgency to the need for teachers to do the same. They cannot opt out of the general relational revolution which our society is now experiencing. More specifically we are therefore saying here that what appear to be the special difficulties of combining in one person the two roles of teacher and counsellor are not special at all. They are simply one facet of a general relational ferment experienced in every walk of life. Schools, industry and business are all faced with management problems which are very similar and the teacher-counsellor role conflict is simply one aspect of them.

If this is true, as I believe it to be, then rigidly to categorize teachers as teachers, and counsellors as counsellors is to move against the general evolutionary trend in other walks of life. We need instead to look at the overlap between the roles, and the extent to which teachers can become counsellors, instead of trying to emasculate a counselling service by fitting it into the sort of relational strait-jacket which is manifested in other educational activities by timetables and subjects. Those who advocate such a rigid categorization are, I believe, stifling human adaptability and fostering fear of the unknown. Rather should we encourage people to look on counselling as a challenge to be met by teachers, just as new management approaches can be seen as challenges by those who are prepared to meet them and new legislation by those who administer the law. Counselling, once again, is about attitudes to other people, as are management methods and legislation. Of course, its special challenge has to be met by in-service selection and training, in the same way that business and industry provide courses for selected people to re-orientate them and help them to face up to new situations. The central fact, however, is that the so-called conflict of roles between teacher and counsellor is simply part of the whole canvas of changing social relationships, not a unique problem in itself, which no other category of society has to face. To realize this is to put the problem in its proper perspective and accord to it its proper dimension; and teachers who take a very restricted instructional view of their job ought to realize this. It may help them to consider re-orientating their attitudes in the direction of counselling.

So far we have looked upon the so-called conflict between the teaching and counselling roles implicitly or explicitly as a state of stress within the practitioner himself. It is easy enough to say that he has to come to terms with this stress, and that the teacher's new counselling role is simply another facet of a wider state of flux in the generality of changing social relationships. This may only conceal a different but very real conflict which is inherent in situations provoked by the two roles. It will help here if we consider a rather exceptional case brought to a teacher-counsellor's attention: that of a student caught by a teaching colleague in the act of stealing school property. This really comprises two situations. The first is the theft itself, which is an offence against the interests of society and of the school community in particular: this teachers have a clear and inescapable duty to sustain. The second is the background of the student and his reasons for committing the offence, an understanding of which is essential to a counsellor's rehabilitatory function. These two situations are in conflict, and it is worth recalling at this stage that this very conflict is an integral part of the legal treatment of offenders under criminal law. Here a balance has to be kept between protecting society and expressing its disapproval on the one hand, and so treating the offender that he becomes a more responsible member of society. That the penal system works very imperfectly in this respect does not deny the existence of the conflict; it only emphasizes the inadequacy of the system.

In a case of this kind, it is easy for a teacher-counsellor to be thrown into confusion by the stress arising within himself unless he first recognizes clearly that this stress stems from the two conflicting situations contained in the case. By understanding the origins of the stress he can begin to live with it and then use his judgement and insight coolly in deciding how to deal with the case presented to him. It does not necessarily follow that such a conflict of situations must produce such a stress within himself that it leads to paralysis of judgement and behaviour disturbance. Whether it does or not depends upon his personality and training. He must, however, be clear that one kind of conflict – the situational – leads to the other – the internal – and that the two kinds exist.

Teachers who are discussing the teacher-counsellor's role for the first time display great interest in cases of this sort. It is, I think, understandable that their immediate reaction is to imagine themselves being paralysed in judgement and action by the impact of such situational conflict. More considered reflection, however, suggests to some of them that such a conflict is tolerable, and that understanding it is in fact a step towards prudent and humane handling of the offender.

It is argued, of course, that the existence of two conflicting situations, provoked by the teacher-counsellor's double role, is the supreme justification for ensuring that one person deals with one situation, and another with the other. In other words this is an argument for the specialist non-teaching counsellor. It is, I believe, dangerous to generalize in this matter. I have involved law-enforcing agencies in the prior interests of the community when dealing with unlawful acts within a school. When the law has taken its course, counselling has been attempted.* The two conflicting situations have been dealt with by the same person. On paper the prospects of successful rehabilitation may seem remote. Experience shows, however, that it is possible in some cases. Success or failure is governed

* See page 86.

by the personality of both offending client and teacher-counsellor, dependent upon the latter's ability to offer a relationship and the former's capacity to respond. We should be careful not to underrate the capacity of such clients to respond even to a relationship which has its origins in a penalty for an illegal act.

Moreover the teacher-counsellor, recognizing and being involved in both the conflicting situations may, with some offenders at least, be better able to help them to understand why they have erred, than a specialist whose view may be more limited. I can only express the view that with some clients, counselling which originates in this way works, but with others it does not.

When all is said and done, however, we should not think that cases which involve law enforcement agencies comprise the principal *raison d'être* of a teacher-counsellor's existence. More familiar and common cases are described on pages 53 and 54. Here the conflicting situations lie in breaches of school rules and courtesy on the one hand, and more general need for personal counselling on the other. The situations are less sharply contrasted but the teacher-counsellor still needs to understand that they exist and why they do, even when his 'disciplinary' role involves him with a simple case of momentary discourtesy caused by the day-to-day irritations which burden us all. Yet, even where proven illegalities by students inside or outside school abound, a teacher-counsellor's unruffled judgement and patient firmness can exert a therapeutic effect on clients in a multiplicity of conflict situations, as well as on the school community as a whole. This is equally true, for example, when he is collaborating with a probation officer who is supervising a student who has broken the law outside school.

The burden of this brief discussion is that teacher-counsellors must be able to recognize conflicts in some situations with which they are confronted, and then to come to terms with them, so that they can use their understanding and judgement coolly. Some situational conflicts may, however, cause serious stress and anxiety within some teachers, but not in others. This is why selecting teacher-counsellors is so important.

We have suggested up to this point that the emergence of the two roles of teacher and counsellor is simply another facet of the general relational ferment in society, that teacher-counsellors must recognize the existence of conflicts in situations which are presented to them by clients, and that whether these situational conflicts cause stress in a teacher is a function of the teacher-counsellor's personality and training. This is a far cry from the suggestion that teaching and counselling are mutually antagonistic and irreconcilable roles. Thus I prefer the word 'duality' to describe side-by-side work in the two roles. This enables us to look much more coolly at the dual role of teacher and counsellor, and then at the so-called triple role of senior teacher-counsellor who has oversight of junior teaching colleagues among his duties. It enables us to examine possible links between the roles.

1 *The dual role*

We can begin an analysis of the dual role by considering the sharpest possible conflict we can imagine between the practice and outlook of the conventional teacher who is a familiar figure, and those of the counsellor. It turns out to be something like this:

Teachers impart information	Counsellors elicit it
Teachers talk	Counsellors listen
Teachers work publicly in the classroom	Counsellors work privately in their offices
Teachers' classroom situations are basically those of conflict	Counsellors' situations are those of partnership
Teachers seek to convert and instruct	Counsellors accept
Teachers employ sanctions of organized society	Counsellors depend on their character and personal influence alone

We can all freely admit that this is a statement of extremes, implying the irreconcilability between teaching and counselling to which I have already referred and upon which I have cast doubt. It is true, however, that some teachers' views on relationships between them and their students are so conservative and rigid that the relaxation, equality and partnership which characterize the counselling relationship are quite intolerable to them even to contemplate. The views of such teachers, however, should not permanently obstruct or condition our thinking about future patterns of relationship between students and teachers. For everyone connected with education, as teacher, administrator or layman knows perfectly well that such an arbitrary classification conceals the real truth about the teaching body as a whole. Between these two extremes there lies a vast number of teachers whose attitudes, characters and practices reveal a slant to those of the counsellor. Indeed some are, as I have said, really counselling already. We would expect this variation to occur, on purely statistical grounds anyway. Those who display some of the counsellor's characteristics will not see the teacher-counsellor role as one purely of conflict. For them the decision to consider counselling as a school activity does not lie in the resolution of a conflict: it is much more one about the relative weight to be given to two overlapping and related aspects of the teacher's job in the 'seventies and later. They do not see the roles as antagonistic; they may see them as complementary. If they do see them thus, then for such people the feasibility of the dual role turns upon understanding the stresses which it may cause. To resolve or live with these stresses becomes then a function of the particular teacher's personality, not a conflict between two mutually exclusive activities.

If, however, teacher-counsellors have their stresses to live with – what of their students? Is it possible for them to accept that members of the staff in their schools can perform two different parts on the same school stage? It has been stated categorically to me that this is surely quite unacceptable to students; that the latter cannot know where they stand with such a duality in their teachers; the latter surely would be guilty of duplicity rather than duality in their student's eyes. This view is not confined to certain groups of teachers; it is held by other people who visit schools in a counselling or advisory capacity. I can only rebut it by examples which, in my experience, demonstrate that the dual role is acceptable to some students, just as it is acceptable to some teachers. From these we can perhaps elicit certain conditions which need to be satisfied before the dual role can be discharged by the same person.

The first concerns a boy, nearly sixteen years old, who came to me in a great anger because someone had made oblique remarks about his home and background. We discussed his feelings about this, and the general truculence and awkwardness which characterized his behaviour at the time, as well as certain domestic difficulties which came to light. Several half-hour interviews took place. After the third one he committed a serious breach of safety regulations in a laboratory which put at risk the safety of the whole class. I punished him for this, because, however strongly I feel about the value of counselling, I also believe that there is some justification for a retributive element in dealing with offenders in school who jeopardize the safety of other people. It would not have surprised me at all if he had not continued with the counselling. My feeling was that he would think I had forgotten about the domestic stresses which were at least part of the cause of his general behavioural cussedness. In counselling terms, I expected him to feel rejected by me. At this point it is important to notice that my worries and anxieties were not injecting themselves into the situation. After all the decision to come or not to come was his – not mine: I was there anyway. We shall return to this again, because the counsellor's anxieties can be a significant factor in the way he does his job. However, the client duly turned up for his next interview, as if nothing untoward had happened. This surprised and interested me so much that I asked him why he had returned after being punished by the same man with whom he had talked in confidence so freely. Did he not feel that I had cast him out or written him off? He was quite unabashed by this and replied, 'Oh, that's all right. The punishment was for something outside what we talked about: you had to do what you had to do, because it was part of your job, but it does not stop us talking now.' We went on to discuss possible connections between the laboratory misconduct and home stress with no trace of embarrassment or resentment. I was clearly counselling in one situation and playing the orthodox schoolmaster in the other: the two activities were clearly demarcated in his mind as well as in mine, although I was at first – and as it turned out – quite unnecessarily worried about his ability to understand and accept this distinction. One facet of this, however, is especially important, that he did not expect me during the counselling sessions to exert the kind of summary or arbitrary authority I had displayed over the laboratory incident. He recognized that he could say what he liked without fear of reprisal in the privacy of counselling; that I would not take exception to anything said by him in that particular context, although I would object strongly to public disorder in class.

In another example a series of very frank confidential discussions with a sixteen- and seventeen-year-old group developed into a series of group-counselling sessions which led to some very blunt speaking on a variety of general and personal problems as well as school relationships. These were informative and useful to the group, including myself. One student in particular was unusually frank and critical, but everyone accepted what he had to say most equably. During the series, however, this student committed, outside the group meetings, some school misdemeanour for which I reprimanded him severely in private – he took this without rancour. Again and somewhat to my surprise, this did not restrict the healthy vigour of his contributions to subsequent group sessions. Reflecting once more my anxieties about this reaction, I asked him why the formal interview and reprimand had not changed his relationships with me in the group. He replied, more articulately than the client in the first example, that the two occasions were completely different and their functions quite discrete. He understood clearly, it appeared, the separation of the two roles I played under two different sets of circumstances. My anxieties seemed to be unjustified.

Several important considerations emerge from these examples and have a considerable bearing on the concept of conflicting roles.

The first is that the students concerned in the quoted incidents had experienced, and apparently appreciated, a counselling role on my part, before they committed the mistakes which compelled me to take some corrective action as a teacher possessing authority. Looking back on these and other similar cases there seems to be an implication common to all of them. This is that the students involved accepted the ordinary teachers' corrective role and whatever consequences for them which flowed from it, because they knew beforehand that I had accepted them in counselling as people who possessed worth anyway. General conclusions should not readily be drawn from such pragmatic experience. It is worth considering seriously, however, that corrective action taken by a teacher-counsellor against his clients for breaches of sense and safety round the school raises no difficulties in the minds of the students concerned. There are two conditions, however, attachable to this surprising situation. The students must have recognized the wider possibilities in the relationship between them and the counsellor, and the teacher-counsellor must be able to live with the duality of his role. There is a possible further conclusion to be tentatively drawn from the situations we have looked at. This is that the counselling approach carries with it a sense of justice and a disinterested concern for people which makes corrective action seem to be fair in the minds of the counsellor's clients who become offenders before him. Moreover such offenders may well be very rare because

E

they appreciate the value of being clients and learn something from counselling. It is perhaps difficult to analyse and understand the mental process by which the two students apparently resolved and accepted the so-called conflict of roles. The fact is that they did so, or appeared to do so.

I say 'appeared to do so' because a second consideration is that to experience the confidential relationship between client and counsellor may, consciously or otherwise, induce in clients a belief that they might 'get away with' the kind of misdemeanour which would otherwise incur some sort of sanction. The reasoning of the two clients just quoted could conceivably take the form 'I know this teacher (the teacher-counsellor) well; he will not punish me because he and I are trying to work my problems out; he must and will protect me: therefore I need not be as careful about my behaviour with other teachers as I should otherwise be.' This is a valid comment, sometimes made by teachers in their initial study of counselling and cognate activities. That a client might develop a feeling of privilege, of being 'above the law' is possibly one of the risks of counselling, and there is no way of avoiding it. On the other hand, we should not exaggerate the risk. It seems reasonable to suppose that a client who justified his misconduct in this way would not return for further counselling after punishment because he would feel that it did not in practice offer him the protection he had expected. Thus, a client's return for further counselling after disciplinary action had been taken against him rather implies that he had not expected protection. Yet even if this conclusion is unjustified, continued counselling enables his counsellor to discuss with him the need for self-control in his general school life as part of the mutual good faith of the client-counsellor relationship. Here teacher-counsellors seem to be very well placed to do this, because they know by current experience the practical problems of class-room control which teachers face. These problems are also part of the client's whole situation, and of the context in which the counsellor works. To believe otherwise is to nullify the whole purpose of counselling, and for a counsellor to exclude a client's classroom experience from counselling is to encourage him to evade one of the realities of his life. It is categorically no part of a counsellor's function to aid and abet such evasion.

Despite this we can never wholly exclude the possibility that some clients might seek to exploit relationships with their counsellors so as to protect themselves from the latter's teaching colleagues. A teacher-counsellor's perceptiveness and judgement are at issue; so too is the quality of his relationships with his teaching colleagues. If this is good, he can not only 'read' his clients perceptively and sensitively, he will be able also to ascertain quietly whether colleagues detect any signs of arrogance or presumption of immunity from sanctions in his clients. It is not even necessary for him to say that he is counselling a particular student. After all, this is simply a slightly more sophisticated version of the normal consultation that goes on in any staff-room between competent and sensitive teachers about the attitudes, application and conduct of pupils. The only limitation is that the counsellor cannot disclose what he has learned in counselling. This informal consultative operation in the client's interests is bound to be facilitated by the fact that the counsellor in this instance also teaches. Beyond this, if it does turn out that a client appears, on the basis of information obtained from teaching colleagues, to be exploiting the relationship with his counsellor, the latter can discuss the classroom maladjustments of his client during counselling as a way of helping the latter's school progress. If this fails to elicit any positive contribution from the client, a teacher-counsellor can confront him with his failure to respond, and tell him that there is no useful purpose in continuing. If this seems drastic we should remember here that several interviews will have elapsed when this stage is reached. To end counselling is the very last resort, however, and teacher-counsellors should not be stampeded into hastily condemning or rejecting a client who has class-room difficulties by the often transient and testy complaints of colleagues who may only be suffering from momentary irritation or liverishness which we all experience at some time. The coolness of judgement, sang-froid and sensitivity of teacher-counsellors should be as valuable in mollifying the exasperations of their colleagues as they are in helping their young clients to maturity. Even so, the point at which to reject a client because he gives nothing to the counselling relationship is an extremely fine one to judge in particular cases, and this is discussed later (p. 84) in a slightly different context.

The third consideration is probably more important, and easier to state clearly. Here at least a clear line can be drawn between the counselling and the teaching role. It is quite simply that a teacher-counsellor cannot start an interview in a counselling capacity (with all that this implies in the terms of what I have said) and, when something is said by a student to which he would take exception if it was uttered in class to him as a teacher, alter his role during the interview by reverting to his teaching image, threatening sanctions for what his client has said, and then expect his young client to accept him in a counselling role once again! The client in such a circumstance will be forgiven if he wonders where on earth he stands and what his alleged counsellor is up to. I have already referred to criticism of my own moods in my earlier experience of counselling, and I have also in my possession written criticism of my uncertainty in this respect from young men with whom I had felt I had a counselling relationship. 'You cannot expect people of my age to know where they stand with you if they cannot be certain about your attitudes and moods as they are revealed by your manner and expression from one day to another or from one hour to another': that about sums up the situation as seen through the eyes and moods of a seventeen-year-old student of mine. It also gives me a chance of discussing coolly the moods of all human beings. We should not expect young men and women to display greater stability of temper and judgement than we do as adults. Significant relationships, which are as we have seen the foundation of counselling, cannot be constructed, and their therapeutic value harnessed, when the counsellor's views of himself and the relationships he develops oscillate suddenly and violently between the roles of co-operative counsellor and the despotic pedagogue in a private interview. If the counsellor does not know where he stands throughout an interview, we cannot expect the client to do so. It is essential to add here that this kind of role-switching inside a single interview is absolutely devastating to the student's view not only of the counsellor, but also of adults in general and what they stand for. It is a breach of faith and few things are more dangerous to young people than breaches of faith on the part of any adult. The special position of teachers as custodians of the young lays a heavy burden of duty upon them in this respect. For them to counsel only accentuates their responsibility as exemplars of stable conduct and personal integrity.

More than one teacher of my acquaintance has voluntarily created for himself something approaching a counselling situation. He has done so by encouraging a young 'client' to involve himself in unrestricted private discussion. Unfortunately he has not realized how deep the involvement would become for the student. In the event a stage was reached in which the teacher's own views and conduct came under fire from the student, who believed in good faith that this was what the man was encouraging and ready to hear calmly. In place of this acceptance, however, the man in each case became very angry and condemned the student for saying what he believed he had been encouraged to say. Demands for apology and threats of sanctions followed. The man's ego was affronted; but more significantly his personal insecurity, fears and anxiety had got the better of him. He did not realize that the subsequent total destruction of the relationship was due to these very causes. Counsellors' anxieties and fears are important: their existence has to be recognized and admitted before living with them becomes tolerable. The teacher in this instance did not recognize, admit or even understand their existence.

At this stage, another illustration may be helpful. Two or three years ago, a sixteen-year-old came out of one of his GCE exams, and waited outside my door 'in something of a state'. I was sent for. I had never taught him: I did not even know his name. However, we did not bother with this, for he was obviously quite upset. He was pale, drawn, confused in speech and very tired. These were perhaps the natural consequences of some weeks of very hard study, and the immediate results of two and a half hours intense concentration during an examination in very hot weather. But he was in no mood to accept these rational and commonsense explanations of a state of mind which almost began to look like a form of mental disorientation. The world was a mess; the system a futility; people were of no importance; there was no point in doing the other six papers which were still to come. No one believed any longer in goodness and kindness; people were going queer, and society was turning upside down. This and many kindred thoughts poured out in a confused flood as time went on. His confusion began slowly to lessen, he became more relaxed, and began to chat rather than ramble. I asked him to come again, which he did and we talked some more about the same sort of topics. In the meantime, I found out discreetly all I could from colleagues who taught him without disclosing the extent of his disturbance or why I was enquiring: he was hardworking, conscientious, rather quiet, absolutely dependable, expected to do well and much respected. He conformed to the school regime and academic system – or so it seemed. Underneath this façade, however, powerful forces seemed to be asserting themselves which no one had suspected. All kinds of information came out in further interviews with him which took place during the next three or four days.

Everything seemed to be going well until some days later he missed an exam one morning and one of his parents appeared asking if he had in fact turned up for it. They were worried about him at home. He had set out from there at the usual time, but he seemed to be unable to communicate with anyone at home and they had begun to wonder what he was going to do. Now parental concern can be very disturbing; there is an emotional involvement which sometimes naturally makes a given situation look worse than it really is. However, at this juncture I began to feel myself pressured by the emotional concern of the parents. I had been concerned about the boy, but not to the extent of alarm or anxiety: I had met cases like this before and he had not seemed to be any more, if as, serious as others. Adolescent moods are often evanescent; but I was sure of one thing, that he would not accept any orders from me as a schoolmaster in the form 'You *must* turn up for the other examination papers'. But now the parents were on the scene, worried about him as their son, about his examination prospects and how his whole future would be affected. We gave them some factual reassurance about this, but the core of the matter was that he was missing. All sorts of rational explanations can be produced when people miss examinations, and there is much to be said here for William of Ockham's dictum that of any solution to a given problem, the simplest is to be preferred until we are certain to the contrary. None the less, the anxiety pressure was on. Had he gone off on his own, run away, or done something more serious? What could be done? Most people quite naturally want to *do* something in a crisis especially when they are emotionally involved. My advice to all concerned was to do nothing and wait. He duly turned up for the afternoon examination on the same day, quite cheerfully. Had he forgotten the morning paper? He had simply lost his timetable, and all he was certain of was the time of the afternoon paper in a subject he liked and the teacher of which he respected. This last comment, if true, suggested perhaps the importance he attached to people and relationships with them. I confess to some feeling of inner relief when he appeared, and then turned up later for all his other papers. For my anxieties had begun to assert themselves, and were probably only mitigated by the fact that there were many other things to do at that time as well as concern myself too much with one young man. There were other school pressures on me, apart from his parents' visit. None the less perhaps something more ought to have been done after his first visit. But what? Had sufficient been said to convince him that he ought to turn up to all his papers? Had we assured him and his parents enough that there were always other chances of doing this examination given a complete return to health? In the light of my experience he was in no state to accept all this. No more could be done. Situations of this kind are bewildering, even frightening, but all one can do is to keep calm and present to the client who is or feels disturbed a serene and welcoming demeanour. This is really the counsellor's function; he must not display his anxieties or resolve them by trying to do something in order to obtain a result, simply to please other people which is the normal reaction of most folk, especially teachers, in such circumstances.

I mention this case at some length because it illustrates with some force the troubles and fears which a counsellor can feel welling up inside him, driving him either to act over-hastily and possibly against his client's best interests, or to opt out of counselling altogether – in other words to funk the issue. This case, together with the examples quoted earlier in this and the preceding chapter, introduces something quite new into the discussion of the feasibility of one person playing the roles both of teacher and of counsellor. We have moved away from the definitive physical or 'mechanical' differences between the teaching and counselling roles. Admittedly these are real enough, and 'in extremes' almost mutually incompatible, but we have suggested two definable conditions which make the duality a sustainable state of affairs. We have also seen that some students at least seem to be able either to accept the difference in the two roles, if they recognize them, or simply not to recognize them. If students either fail to recognize the difference, or take no notice if they do so, why do teachers and other adults concerned with education tend to emphasize them, often in advance of practical experience?

The new factor we now introduce into the discussion is the personality of the teacher who involves himself in the dual role. This is the factor which led me to lay such emphasis in *Teachers as Counsellors* on selecting the most suitable people for the dual role. Now personality is a collective term covering many aspects of the behaviour of a particular individual, but I want to draw attention to two in particular; security and anxiety which I have already touched upon.

In commonsense terms, I suppose most people would think of security as a feeling of safety, of unassailability in whatever they are doing, or that the state in which they are living is unlikely to be shaken easily. I do not mean by security, a sense of smugness, complacency or self-satisfaction. These are the very negation of a counsellor's qualities and it is possible to feel secure without feeling complacent, although I suppose the one could quite easily be transformed into the other in the total absence of that self-critical quality which is another necessary attribute of a counsellor. Security in the sense in which I would use it in the present context connotes a state of inner peace, personal serenity and harmony within one's self, a state which predicts freedom from inner tensions and serious conflicts. Such security confers upon the person who possesses it an ability to face people, problems and situations with an equanimity which has its foundation in that person's integrity. Such a security implies the possession of an underlying philosophy of living which is a stabilizing influence.

When they use the word anxiety most people think of worry or concern about themselves or others, while the word has a more sophisticated meaning in the language of psychotherapy. I am not using it here in any other than the general common-sense one. The three examples in this chapter, and the group situations described in the preceding one both included references to my own feelings about my ability to cope with the counselling situation, the stresses created by it, my client's reactions to the switch of roles, outside influences or any combination of these. I emphasize that it is my – the counsellor's – anxieties (for this is the word we can now use) about myself and my clients and their situations, not theirs about me, which are important at this stage of the discussion. How then do we live with these anxieties if we are involved in both counselling and teaching?

The first part of the answer is to recognize that the anxieties exist. The second is to realize that they may be exacerbated by the likelihood that a pure teacher may resolve any given situation in one way, but a counsellor does it in another. This is implied in the original contrast between the two roles. This recognition and realization are counselling imperatives, for if we are not aware of the problem we cannot deal or live with it. One reason for postulating continuous in-service training for counsellors is the maintenance of this awareness.

It is a very easy escape from one's own difficulties to say that someone is the cause of them. Of course, this is sometimes true – but certainly not always. If we return to the case of the boy who missed an examination, it would be easy to blame the presence of anxious parents for my own worries. The truth is that they were there, I was anxious and most people would think, quite naturally; but my function was to help the parents to live with *their* worries, to give them some serenity, not to display my own and thus make their situation worse. At the time they came there was nothing that could be 'done'. Students have missed examinations before; my experience of other boys in like states – and there are enough who crack under examination strain to give abundant experience – did not suggest that this particular student was really going to have a mental breakdown. Therefore, calmness, living with the anxieties was all that was possible for the moment. This was the reality of the situation: and it is reality with which counsellors must all live, not escape from it into a dream world or by rushing about doing things which are really irrelevant at the given time.

The trouble is that no one can tell another person that he must live with his anxieties. Some people can: they ought to come through a selection process. Others can be orientated to do so by a combination of selection and training. Yet others simply cannot: they should not even think about counselling.

Recognition of the anxieties, must, however, come first and this is probably more difficult to come to than is the ability to live with them. If we do not recognize their existence and how they influence our judgement, then the latter may be confused by mental processes which we do not necessarily understand. For this reason, continuous in-service training for counsellors, supporting discussion groups and specialized agencies to which reference can be made are imperatives for teacher-counsellors, and indeed for specialist counsellors.

At this stage let us summarize the probable conditions which so far I believe need to be satisfied before the dual role of teacher and counsellor can be properly sustained by one person.

a. The teacher-counsellor is seen by his clients as a counsellor first. It seems easier for a client to accept correction from one who counselled him, than it is for a student to initiate counselling with the person who has corrected him first. In the latter case much depends upon the temperament of the student, for students aged eleven or twelve may well be corrected by a teacher but come to him as a counsellor when they are sixteen or seventeen, and be surprised by the changes in themselves during the five or six years.

b. Teacher-counsellors must keep their roles separate in the sense that once they have embarked upon counselling in private, they cannot during the interviews assume the role of the authoritarian teacher, although they may do so in the public glare of the class-room.

c. Teacher-counsellors need to feel secure, but not complacent; they need calm and integrated personalities so that they can endure stress.

d. Teacher-counsellors must be able to recognize and live with the stresses and anxieties of the counselling role. It is not easy, but it is manageable, given in-service support. We shall return to this point later.

e. Teacher-counsellors must undergo a selection process and have continuous in-service training and support.

We have already suggested that the duality in the teacher-counsellor's activities is not confined to education alone, that it is extending to industry and commerce and other activities. Before I leave this duality two more aspects of it may help further to put it into a proper perspective. First, the duality afflicts us all. Everyone clings to some extent to the past while looking forward tentatively into an uncertain future. In teaching we still persist with old methods knowing that new knowledge drives us reluctantly to look at new methods; we hang on desperately to familiar practices in ecclesiastical worship, in the consciousness that we fail to hold or attract or influence people by doing so; we look nostalgically at social customs which give an ephemeral security, although we know that innovation is inexorable. This is human history really. In the scientific field duality is everywhere: energy and matter, particles and waves. It is not the duality of the teacher-counsellor's role which is unique, it is the ability of the practitioners in this particular field of duality to recognize it, and understand and live with the problems it may present. I am reminded of a much respected chemistry colleague, who was told that a golf ball could be regarded not as a solid sphere but as a wave form. Although possessing a versatile and receptive mind this was too much. 'I give up,' he said, 'My imagination boggles. Golf balls are golf balls!' If the presentation of the counselling face of the dual role provokes this reaction in teachers, they should stick to teaching. It will be better for their clients anyway.

Secondly, the dual role of the teacher-counsellor has a general resemblance to the duality which has to be displayed by most parents. Whether all parents perform their various roles well, or at all, whether indeed the family as we know it is likely to be a continuing viable social unit are both beside the point here. For if parents become increasingly inadequate, teachers will find themselves taking over their role more and more: and if they become more competent, their example will remain a precedent for the teacher's new duality. Parents, if they do their job well, play multiple not dual roles: they have to be friend and guide, private confidant, law enforcers, even punishers, if the situation demands it. Their children accept these roles, because each of them is a manifestation of care and concern, which are also the stock-in-trade of the teacher-counsellor as he faces his clients in private. Here then is but a further example of the duality which affects us all, in society, in knowledge, in history, in the family. Not everyone in these areas of community activity can cope with the duality. So too not every teacher can be able to cope with the teacher-counsellor's role, but this is not a justification for assuming that the two roles are always irreconcilable opposites rather than complementary aspects of a total concern for human beings in the environment of schools.

2 *The triple role*

This term is used to describe the situation in which a teacher-counsellor who holds a senior position of responsibility in a school, has not only to teach and to counsel in the manner outlined in preceding pages, but also as part of his responsibility has a duty to support and guide junior colleagues in class-room control and their relationships with students. He has three roles to discharge, not just two. It is a situation potentially applicable not only to heads of schools but also to their deputies, to year and house masters and heads of subject departments, any of whom may counsel. In it the stresses of counselling students and supporting colleagues, and the tensions between the counsellor's personal loyalty to his clients and professional loyalty to his colleagues, are highlighted. At first sight it is a circumstance which presents insuperable difficulties: yet if counselling is to be undertaken by experienced teachers who have shown themselves masters of their day-to-day craft before becoming counsellors, it could well become a quite common situation.

At the outset the position of heads of schools vis-à-vis coun-

selling presents few difficulties. It is for them to decide whether
they can or will counsel. They alone are responsible for any
consequences: they cannot unload blame or praise on to
anyone else. No managerial problem of selection, delegation
or organization exists. Heads of small schools have counselled,
and will continue to counsel if they feel like doing so. Those
who do so know what it means: no problem of confidentiality
exists because they receive the information personally, and
they know their way round the supporting agencies. I do not
intend therefore to discuss the special position of counselling
headmasters any further. The difficulties arise when schools
become so big that it is physically impossible for one person
to do all the work of this kind, and it has therefore to be delegated to subordinate members of staff.

In discussing this situation as it applies to assistant teachers
we should understand that what has been said of the dual role
applies with equal force to the triple one. Moreover, some part
of what follows has also a connection with the dual role, which
I have only discussed in the restricted context of a straight-
forward resolution of the dilemmas, real or imagined, between
the roles of teacher and counsellor. This is especially true of
the three conditions which must be satisfied if the triple role
is to be sustainable without ill-effects upon the staff, the
students or the counselling teacher. The first of these is that the
head of the school concerned must believe in the value of
counselling as an educational service in the broad sense of
helping their students' personalities and potentialities to
develop to the full. Such a belief necessarily has elements of
faith and trust in it: indeed, if these are missing from the
relationship between a head and his counselling staff the
counselling service itself must be jeopardized. The teacher-
counsellor's roles, be they dual or triple have little hope of
relaxed, still less successful, activity when such faith is lacking.
Moreover, if counselling is looked upon as a useful front to
give an impression of up-to-dateness, or has in any other way
merely lip service paid to it, counsellors' services are rendered

nugatory. Hostility, mistrust and doubt are not really desirable parts of a counsellor's working environment. He has enough difficulty without them.

The second condition follows from the first and is virtually an extension of it. This is that the trust between a head and his governors on the one hand and the counsellors on the other must be such that he can say in public, as one headmaster much experienced in this kind of personal education said quite categorically, 'I do not want to know what goes on in discussion between the staff involved and their student clients, unless both counsellor and student, in any given case, voluntarily involve me at a point which seems important and relevant to them.' It is worth noting here that this man was an advocate of very rigorous selection of teachers for counselling. Readers may notice the contrast between the attitude of this man and the view of the headmaster quoted in the introduction, who felt that everything which transpired in counselling must be revealed to him simply because counselling took place on school premises. The motives for this restrictive attitude are obscure, but in fairness to the person concerned he seemed to be somewhat overwhelmed by the novelty of the counselling relationship and unduly sensitive to the stresses it seemed likely to create. This perhaps was natural in a man whose whole teaching life, as he later revealed, had been spent in tough schools with severe disciplinary problems. Most of us would agree that to sit for long periods on such a metaphorical powder-barrel is scarcely calculated to engender the serenity and personal security which counselling demands. This in turn inhibits a rational appraisal of its value.

The third condition is a development of the others. A head must communicate openly with the non-counselling members of his staff, with governors, parents and responsible local authority administrators. He must impart to all these not only his belief and trust in counselling as an activity, but also in the staff who are likely to be involved in it, as well as giving them some idea of how it is to be administered in the school. A service, which by its very nature is private and personal and is dependent upon good faith between counsellor and client, requires the existence of similar trust between the other echelons of the total network of relationships in which the head and counsellor work. This dispels, as far as is possible, any suspicion on the part of non-counselling teachers that their counselling colleagues are liable to exacerbate their own control problems. Proper communication ensures that counsellors are seen as professional colleagues working towards the same end as purely instructional teachers but in a different way, and in that way helping to create the very conditions under which the instructional goals of the school may be the better fulfilled.

Unfortunately however, at the present stage in the growth of counselling services in this country, many heads of schools do not hold the enlightened and trusting view quoted in an earlier paragraph. Certainly the *cris de cœur* of a number of teachers interested in counselling have been such as to suggest that they felt obstructed by the conservative attitudes of their heads, and by their reluctance to take what they were reported to believe was a rather dangerous plunge. At a time when school discipline is thought to be falling this is perhaps natural: it may equally be regarded as a good reason for not looking at new approaches. Be this as it may, it is pertinent to digress for a moment and consider possible reasons for heads' opposition, explicit or implicit, to counselling techniques. In the first place heads of schools have been accustomed in the past to deal confidentially on their own with the private problems and personal disturbances of students. In this respect counselling is not a new experience for some of them at least. This has enabled them to keep firm personal control of situations which might otherwise have got out of hand, in the old-fashioned disciplinary sense. It is not an exaggeration to state that some of them have certainly been counselling genuinely, with great compassion and patience. Some of them, too, would resent the idea that this function should pass out of their hands into those of someone else on the staff. This reluctance to delegate, or to admit that others might perform the same task better, is a personality trait not restricted to heads of schools, however. The sheer size of modern comprehensive schools none the less compels them to do so; and the heads of such large schools have no alternative, in managerial terms alone, to accepting the principle and the fact that they must have subordinates who can perform counselling functions at least as well as they would do so themselves. Size and complexity must bring trust and dependence in their train. Whatever the size of a school, however, every head takes some sort of interest in what is going on and one of the difficulties associated with a counselling service is not so much that other people rather than he himself are making the all-important relationships, but that these are bound by the counsellor's seal of confidence so that he cannot disclose details or even names to him. This is not always a question of heads 'snooping': it is often a simple question of natural concern either for the school in general or people in particular. Here one of the great advantages of the triple role emerges clearly, for it is indubitably easier for a senior teacher who is engaged in counselling to maintain the privacy of his counselling when his head makes enquiries, than it is for a staff junior. The latter, no matter how skilled and understanding a counsellor he may be, will find the stress which his head's enquiries produce in him greater than that in a senior staff member. This in turn may affect his counselling. The relationship between the senior man or woman, and his head is based upon respect born of experience for his judgement and skill as a teacher, and his qualities as a person. This relationship is not one which has necessarily grown easily or rapidly; like the counselling relationship itself it takes no account of hierarchical position, but is based upon a sensible and shrewd appreciation of one another's virtues, so that the head trusts his senior confidants and the latter know he does so. Under these conditions of mutual trust, a counsellor service can flourish. Moreover, the senior man is less likely to be influenced by considerations of future promotion prospects than a younger one whose pro-

F

fessional future has still to be determined. While counselling has its idealistic side, younger teachers like other young people are partly influenced by financial prospects; a feeling that their professional futures would be affected adversely by avoiding replies to their heads' enquiries would almost inevitably affect adversely their poise and serenity in counselling, and hence their interest and involvement.

Secondly, heads who appear to be obstructive or reluctant may well have proper doubts about the personal integrity and overall suitability for counselling of members of their staffs. This is a thoroughly prudent view to take. Teachers who express resentment about the attitudes of their heads are not necessarily suitable counselling material. Indeed the vehemence of their views itself suggests a certain intolerance of ideas they do not share, and this in its turn does not augur well for their ability to handle anxious or angry clients. It simply does not follow that because a teacher feels enthusiastic about counselling he is necessarily fitted to be a counsellor. Enthusiasm might indicate a desire to meddle in other people's affairs because this satisfies some emotional desire in the counsellor. Moreover, there are occasions when a counsellor must break off the relationship with his client unless he is specifically asked not to. If, for example, a client is handed on to a child-guidance specialist, the latter must be the judge of whether the counsellor in school should continue his relationship with the client. The mental and social health of the client is the issue, not the curiosity or emotional needs of the counsellor who referred the case in the first instance. If counsellors, when circumstances demand it, cannot gracefully retire from a case which they have referred, they should really not be counselling at all. As we shall see in referral, however, there is a great deal to be said for the specialist keeping the referring counsellor in touch with developments, as a matter of courtesy and interest. In considering the behaviour of school counsellors in these and similar circumstances we are emphasizing once again the selection of counsellors of the right personal quality. Heads who are cautious in their approach to counselling for these and similar reasons are performing their proper duty, and doing so much more sensibly than those who espouse the cause of counselling with blind enthusiasm or in a desire to impress those to whom they are responsible.

The third reason is that there are some heads, a dying breed one would think, who simply do not believe that counselling performs any useful purpose which is not at least as well performed by the traditional directive but gentle guidance which for generations they have given to their charges. They see little virtue in the decline of imposed authority, believe that their age, experience and position give them the right to instruct young men and women, certainly in their careers and further education. More personal matters are not within their province. Many of us, even counsellors, may at times have felt this too, and regretted the passing of an age when orders were obeyed without question. Such considerations are, however, now irrelevant; for the general tone of the society in which we now live, the vast range of choices which confront youngsters, the moral decisions they have to make, the uncertainty of social values – all these make the old imperatives virtually outdated, if only because, as far as schools are now concerned, there is scarcely any sanction which can enforce compliance. Heads in this category, however, badly misjudge the situation if they believe that counselling has become important because sanctions have failed. There are many reasons for it, not the least being that younger people express a need for it: hence schools must provide the discerning and caring adults to whom the youngsters can turn if it transpires in certain cases that the counsellors' function is simply to assist their clients to talk about what used to be imposed upon them without reason.

In essence, heads reject or are cautious about counselling for as many reasons or combinations of them as there are heads. No one can compel heads of schools to introduce a counselling service against their better judgements, even if they have among their staff one or two teachers who are both interested and

suitable. Heads have to make the appropriate decision themselves; it is for them alone to make a thorough assessment of
whatever evidence and experience is available to them in
making that decision. All heads have abundant worries anyway
and some of them certainly feel that counselling services will
only add to their already considerable burdens. Neither
administrative fiat nor educational fashion should bring them
to change their minds: the most influential factor for them to
consider is whether they might not find that trusting the
judgement of carefully selected colleagues would in fact reduce
their personal worries and alleviate some of the burden
which they now carry as well as serve their students' needs. In
particular, selecting and training members of staff whose relationships and reputations are already known and trusted
within a school would seem to offer greater opportunities of
help to such heads. The relationship of such teachers with their
students, their integrity, poise and balance are known to be
first class, by comparison with the personal qualities of out-
siders who are unknown quantities. With them trusting relationships cannot be created simply by appointing them as counsellors. Good relationships and healthy reputations have to grow
within a school: they cannot be manufactured. Similarly, heads
of schools have to 'grow' new attitudes to counselling as
experience is shared and information is spread.

Establishing these general relational conditions does not, of
course, automatically eliminate all possibilities of difficulty and
friction in a counselling service. Human beings simply do
not work that way – not even counsellors, although, of all
people, they might be expected to be free from uneasy relationships. We have now to look at the day-to-day incidents which
might be expected to make life a little difficult for one who tries
to play the triple role, as well as for the whole nexus of relationships within a school. Let us therefore consider one example
of the practical problems which beset the triple role player and
see how that role can be discharged in practice. I ought to add
here that the ensuing account is based upon an actual case,

not upon a hypothetical situation. Gubbins was near the end of his fourth year. He was no genius but he had a modicum of ability, which he employed minimally and according to his likes and dislikes of teachers and subjects. He was a large, awkward, raw-boned youth, bereft of any polish. It was difficult to assess in advance his performance in any external examination, and he appeared not to consider the prospect of taking one seriously anyway. He knew well how to disturb people, however, in class, when he was in one of his frequent intractable moods. Mr 'A' was his current victim and brought him before higher authority for correction. Higher authority happened to be a senior member of the staff, Mr 'X', who was also a counsellor. We shall notice here that Gubbins was brought, not sent, to Mr 'X'. Justice is seen to be done this way, since both parties to the dispute heard the statement of complaint and any defence against it. This element of justice is a vital one in the work of any teacher-counsellor. Gubbins was obviously a rather rough diamond who 'played up' Mr 'A' with a variety of well-known schoolboy's devices and exercised a baleful influence over others. His work, if done, was late in delivery; he talked quietly but incessantly in class; he was an expert in the well-known gentle art of surreptitious furniture removal in class, making just enough noise to annoy or irritate but rarely enough to create a definable incident. He had never actually been rude to Mr 'A' in class, but the latter felt he was coming very close to doing so. It was not so much what he said, or did not say, but the manner in which he did so. There was a touch of 'dumb insolence' about him. The culprit admitted all this in front of Mr 'A' and Mr 'X'. He knew probably that he had almost got Mr 'A' 'on the run', and that the latter did not know what to do. This last was very true, for Gubbins was a big strong fellow, who seemed to wield a certain amount of influence among a group of sycophantic admirers with similar backgrounds but less cunning. Mr 'A' wanted him corrected, at least partly because he was slightly frightened, but he did not know how to do so. Hence his arrival at Mr 'X's door in the belief that 'higher authority' would do the trick. Mr 'X' was now in the standard counsellor's dilemma, but with Mr 'A' to cope with as well. He had a professional loyalty to his colleague; he also knew that Gubbins' disruptive influence if allowed to pass unheeded could spread beyond this master's class-room all over the school. He had met this implied threat earlier as a teacher himself long before he started counselling. It was a possibility to be considered seriously, counselling or no counselling. Moreover he knew too that he himself could not counsel in the midst of sheer chaos. On the other hand his counselling self wanted to know why the youth did the things of which he had been accused and to which he had admitted. He was also 'an old hand' and certainly not at all frightened by the lanky 15¾-year-old before him or by his associates.

Mr 'X' asked Mr 'A' to leave the matter with him. He would report back in due course. He went on to enquire further of Gubbins what this was really all about. At this stage, however, let us consider for a moment how the young man might have been feeling. He had never been taught by or talked to the senior man before. All he knew was that he had been brought before him in expectation of some sort of punishment—at least Mr 'A' had led him to believe this. Yet, all that was happening was that Mr 'X' was 'chatting him up'. It was possibly very confusing for Gubbins; he did not know what was going to happen, and as he was heard to say later to one of his mates he did not know 'whether he was comin' or goin' '. He was not at all confident about the outcome of the chat in which he was at the moment engaged. Indeed he may have thought that he was being 'conned'. This, too, was a thought, at this stage, which might have been passing through the counsellor's mind as he tried to break through to the rough, taciturn, semi-hostile young man before him, about whose motives and attitudes little was known.

Step by step a picture of Gubbins' attitude and situation emerged through patient questioning and most relevant answers. His harassment of Mr 'A' had been going on for some time, but in his view this was only retaliation against this man's constant attempts, as he saw them, to make a fool of him in front of the class. Mr 'A' was savage with his tongue at times, and scorned rougher boys who did not take to his subject. Gubbins took as poor a view of him as he did of the boy. Neither cared for the other in any meaning of the phrase. Each seemed to think the other had no right to exist, but the man had the advantage because he could say all this better. Gubbins found it difficult to reply appropriately and reverted to sullen silence and then in the ways which prompted his mentor to bring him down to Mr 'X'. Mr 'A' felt that his authority in his class-room was beginning to falter. For him this was a most unsatisfactory situation, and correction of some kind was necessary to buttress him.

The senior man's problem was now clarifying. If only he alone had been involved there would be no doubt that he would simply continue counselling, but he had both to support and invoke the aid of Mr 'A' in this case, because the latter's feelings were important too. They were part of the whole context. Mr 'X' knew quite a lot about his colleague. In particular he was aware of his methods and his attitude to his job, both of which were in general thoroughly professional, even if a little orthodox. Yet, he knew from his own teaching experience with tougher characters than Gubbins that arbitrary punishment was not necessarily the best or the only way of dealing with the kind of situation Mr 'A' had presented. It might have been an effective fashion forty years ago, but this is in itself no proof that it is now either right in general principle or appropriate in a particular case. The preliminary enquiry had only revealed a continuing pattern of mutual hostility between Gubbins and Mr 'A'. Was there something more to Gubbins' attitude? If it could be 'dug out' perhaps Gubbins could be encouraged to prevent himself heading towards a sort of scrapheap. So he was invited back for a further talk. Nothing so far had happened to Gubbins and, in the vernacular, he now had no idea at all 'what the score was'. Before the youth returned at the time set, Mr 'X' told Mr 'A' as a matter of courtesy that he was extending his investigation into the offender's behaviour. In succeeding interviews it turned out that the youth had a background which was rather discouraging: neither parent helped in any sense, but were not hostile; his out-of-school associates rather reviled him for wearing the blazer he wore, and the only people he had any respect for on the staff were those who treated him as a man. The formal intellectual approach to work seemed to be beyond him, but even that was tolerable if the staff who taught the more academic subjects treated him properly. Mr 'A's combination of intellectual superiority and personal contempt was however too much for this particular youth, especially when he had no point of contact with his parents, and his mates outside school did not think much of schools and learning anyway.

Upon reflection, I suppose, there is really nothing very extraordinary about this situation in school life. The issue was not the problem but the solution, and in pursuit of this Mr 'X' then saw Mr 'A' again, explained that he had found out something about Gubbins, and that the latter clearly had some problems to cope with. Could Mr 'A' see his way perhaps to be helpful and encouraging sometimes rather than always critical and derogatory? Mr 'A' was, happily, co-operative and grateful. Gubbins was also brought face to face with the fact that just as Mr 'A' had to put up with him, so too had he to put up with Mr 'A'. Both of them existed. Gubbins did not like this idea much. However, Mr 'X' suggested that if he found this difficult to live with, it would perhaps be a good idea for him to come and talk to Mr 'X' whenever he felt that relations with Mr 'A' were becoming too much for him to stand. One other thing was important for Gubbins to understand: there were other fellows in the class who might just want to get on with their work and they might find him something of a nuisance. It would be sensible for him to remember them when he felt angry and resentful. Moreover, Mr 'A' would be expected to report to Mr 'X' if there were any more outbreaks of trouble with this student. Gubbins appeared not to like this overmuch, but for the moment the matter was left there to see how relationships with Mr 'A' developed. Certain features of the case are worth noting, however, at this point in its development.

The senior teacher-counsellor was trying to improve communication between the offender and the offended. This seemed to him to be the crux of the matter. He looked upon summary punishment at this stage as detrimental to his efforts. He was not undermining his teaching colleague's disciplinary position, although he had not done exactly what the colleague wanted. He was in constant communication with him as both professional courtesy and counselling required. Mr 'A' also retained his own right to administer whatever punishment lay within his power. The counselling senior teacher was not intervening in or taking over Mr 'A's class control: that was still for him to work out for himself, as every teacher has always had to do. The crux of the matter, however, was the relationship between the teacher who sought guidance and the man who gave it to both student and teacher, in which the general status and character of the senior man were also important factors. As long as he kept calm, both his colleague and the student would tend to cool down, thus lowering the social temperature to the point at which all could consider for themselves what was best for the youth in the case. The optimum course for the youth was the overriding goal. We must try to find that out in every case. It might in the long run have turned out that some kind of condign punishment was necessary and the counsellor had reserved the right to administer it, in support of the whole school regime, counselling-orientated as it was, but he had used his counselling skill first.

It is arguable that something of a mountain has been made out of a molehill in this instance. Why on earth should this kind of simple action be supererogated into counselling? But this is exactly what it is because Mr 'X' has accepted Gubbins with all his faults and failings as a human being with a dignity of his own, and he has started with him as he is. The description of the incident and immediately ensuing action may indeed make it sound much more long-winded than it really was in practice. Similar cases rarely take more than one or two interviews to achieve some kind of short-term stability in a deteriorating situation, regardless of any long-term follow-up. Mr 'X' behaved rather more perceptively in his handling of an errant pupil than a conventional senior master who simply administers punishment after a merely formal enquiry. Upon his shoulders, too, lay the responsibility for following up the case, by seeing Gubbins from time to time and maintaining the link with him; and by talking with Mr 'A' to support him in tolerating the fellow he did not like very much. It is arguable too, that this was a very time-consuming operation. So it was, and there is a limit to the amount of time which can and should be spent upon an individual case. This, however, is always a matter of judgement on the counsellor's part. I shall come back to the problem of time in the final chapter – for this obviously concerns interested teachers, but it is really an administrative problem.

One criticism of what seems to be a rather laborious means of handling a simple and common school matter is that it may not for more than a week or two alter Gubbins' conduct at all, even when Mr 'A' co-operates. If this were true it would imply a total lack of sensitivity on Gubbins' part to the feelings of everyone else. It would also signify a species of failure on Mr 'X's part. What constitutes failure or success is very hard to define. We shall turn to failure again shortly, but for the moment let us assume that Mr 'X' had not managed to obtain *any sort* of co-operation from the boy, by his counselling approach. If this were indeed so then it would have been, in my experience, extremely unusual, and would indicate that there was something deeper amiss in the young client's behaviour pattern. In such a case the co-operation of the parents should be sought in order to obtain more expert advice, for example from the local authority's psychological guidance service, to ascertain whether there is something very seriously wrong with the boy. We shall return to this point in the chapter on referral.

A second criticism of this case is that it does not suggest what should be done if Mr 'A', the original complainant, had insisted on punishment because he found the slower-moving methods of the counsellor, despite the latter's seniority, quite intolerable. Although he really handed the problem to Mr 'X', he had, of course, a right to go over the counsellor's head, as it were, to the head of the school, in an endeavour to obtain what he believed was satisfaction, i.e. summary punishment. At such a juncture, any headmaster's management of a counselling service is critical. If he has not previously made clear the trust which he placed in his counselling staff then he must expect to face, at some stage in such a case, a serious dispute between two people. In the quoted case one of these would have been the experienced and senior counselling teacher, a key man on the staff whose loyalty to him and the school was beyond question. He would have been fully entitled to complain with vigour about what he believed to be the thoroughly unprofessional attitude of a trusted colleague who went above him without talking the matter over openly once more. We might think under these circumstances that any teacher who behaved so discourteously needed counselling himself, because he was an adult showing precisely the symptoms which the young client displayed – namely a high level of concern with himself alone. Clearly, however, such a situation would place an additional stress upon the counsellor, who must at all costs maintain his own calm and serenity, even in the face of such a display of adult self-indulgence. The best and proper procedure here would be for Mr 'A' and Mr 'X' and the headmaster to have a case conference at which they discuss the young man's case calmly, and come to an agreed decision.

We should be frank about this. A single case scarcely disposes of all the difficulties besetting the man or woman who attempts the triple role. Yet a detailed study of every case in my own experience would achieve little more. Counsellors cannot depend upon the minutiae of known cases for detailed guidance in those with which they have yet to be confronted. They are not lawyers depending upon legal precedents, or scientists upon their experimental procedures. Rather, they depend upon their own integrity, experience and sensitivity; for these are among the components of that clear perception and acute judgement which often enable them to decide what course to follow in any given case. It may be argued that what I have described in these pages is simply what many headmasters and their senior teachers do already, given comparable situations. If this is indeed true then there are more natural untrained counsellors at large than our school system is given credit for. Before we agree with acclamation that all senior and head teachers are counsellors, however, we should pause and think again about what Mr 'X' was trying to achieve in the quoted case. He was not just trying to plaster over a crack in the disciplinary structure of the school, and that of Mr 'A's classroom in particular, by a rather paternalistic chat-up. He was deliberately, and perhaps at some risk to his reputation, refusing to exploit the special authority of his position in an attempt to get Gubbins to talk freely and privately about his own feelings and reasons for his conduct. He hoped that some kind of relationship might thus be formed between him and the boy which would help the latter to find, even on a limited scale, a self-control which might make school more tolerable for him than it appeared to be, and to understand his whole wider personal situation better.

By listening *to* Gubbins, rather than talking *at* him he hoped that he might come to the point at which he could tolerate Mr 'A' at first in the immediate future, and subsequently for a longer period. Although this was clearly what Mr 'A' hoped for, it was only part of the wider purpose which Mr 'X' had in mind – that of helping him to come to terms with himself and the reality of his situation. Neither of these wider aims are necessarily achievable in cases of this kind, by the well-known, friendly, but unmistakably authoritative chats which are the stock-in-trade of a great many heads and senior teachers in what they would call disciplinary situations. These do not approach the true counsellor's efforts really to understand the student in the case, and to help him to come to terms with a personal situation which is a fact of life. Avuncular, paternalistic or condescending chats, however good their intentions, are an attempt to impose by a sort of kindness an acceptance of reality upon the student. They do not help him to come to it himself.

Let us return again to the Gubbins affair which was, however, not yet over. He certainly managed to tolerate Mr 'A' and the latter him. The confrontation subsided permanently into a mutually suspicious and utterly futile relationship. Thereafter he never got into any real trouble elsewhere in the school. His almost passionate dedication to sporting service to the school continued, but this remained the only bright spot on an otherwise dark picture. He became exceptionally self-contained, locking himself up in a suit of psychological armour-plate which no one seemed to be able to penetrate. He seemed to be able to maintain a continuous silent resentment of the school, its staff and older students. He was never upbraided in public by anyone on the staff, but even the most sensitive among them began to wish that he would just complain about something, of his own volition. His parents visited the school to discuss his future. They were keen for him to stay on, and begrudged nothing to that end, partly belying the impression he had given of them, but they did not see that they had a positive part to play. His very self-contained attitude was a puzzle to them as it was to all who met him in school. He became one of those people who create an aura of mystery, or even menace, about them. Everyone wondered whether, when or how he would explode out of his shell with some kind of seriously anti-social act.

In all, he never really responded to the counselling approach as far as could be seen in school, in the sense of contributing something to it himself or relaxing just a little or co-operating positively, still less of realizing just as others like him had, the

possibilities which the school offered to him as a person –
sporting activities apart. He would not give an inch. He never
went to see Mr 'X' unless he was asked; and counselling him
was extremely hard work for Mr 'X'. He never displayed any
sensitivity to the feelings of other people, or understanding of
their needs, staff or students alike. If there was any medium
– or long-range – achievement of the kind of social well-being
and personal ease which everyone hoped and watched for, it
was not seen in school. In particular he retained his ability to
lie and tell half-truths, which demanded constant vigilance from
the staff.

In the event, he got himself into trouble outside the school,
and he passed into the hands of other agencies. Whether he
recovered from this eventually was not known to the school.
Unhappily this event anticipated an intended referral by the
school to the local authority's psychological service. This would
have been intended to find out whether he was disturbed, or
just a very lonely character who resented adult authority, and
why. Perhaps this should have been done earlier, but the
relevant evidence was slight and indefinable and prospects of
parental co-operation were poor. It would have been based on
very uncertain feelings about him. Perhaps also, he might have
been given earlier what the courts call a short sharp shock to
bring him up against reality with a jolt by punishment. This
might have led him to see that some modification of his attitude
was needed. Depriving him of his sport could possibly have
helped to this end. He might have responded to a different counsellor, because Mr 'X' was perhaps too closely associated with
authority in his mind to be a good counsellor for him. If this was
so then Mr 'X' must bear some responsibility for the misad-
ventures which subsequently befell him. On the other hand no
one on the staff had made any relationship with him at all and
very serious attempts were made to achieve this, not only by the
counsellor. Moreover, Mr 'X' had been successful with other
students with comparable backgrounds and histories not only
in terms of plain personality development but also, in some

cases, of remarkable intellectual accomplishment. He might have responded to a resident non-teaching counsellor. Here again, however, there was a strong feeling on the staff that he would have exploited skilfully any differences which could well have arisen between counsellor and teaching staff, using the former as an umbrella to protect himself against the latter.

All this, of course, is speculation in retrospect, with whatever understanding hindsight brings. At the time, the approach used was thought to be the appropriate one. Despite the analysis afterwards, when it is so easy to be wise, I would not personally treat any similar case differently, but looking back on it is valuable because it reminds us all of the potential complexities of any counselling situation. It also highlights the special problems and considerations attachable to the triple role: the need for good management of counselling within a school; trust between head, senior teaching-counsellors and staff; constant communication between counselling and non-counselling staff involved in a given case; the counsellor's judgement and patience in trying to preserve a balance between maintaining communication with his client and helping the latter to see the value of other people in his community, as the counsellor saw value in him. For Gubbins was never 'written off' by Mr 'X' despite the problems he presented and his own problems of retaining staff support while considering his client's needs.

Given the conditions of trust and communication, the triple role is manageable. It is sustainable too if the senior staff member who sustains it is recognized by his non-counselling colleagues as a thoroughly competent teacher and controller of boys, quite apart from his skill in the privacy of the counselling room. If the one student's case which we have discussed could be recorded as inconclusive, other students have responded to a person who discharged the triple role. The Gubbins episode does not suggest that this role is quite impracticable: rather does it direct our attention to the problem of so-called 'failure' in counselling. The failure to evoke any response from a client is perhaps a more searching crisis for the senior teacher-counsellor performing three roles than it is for a practitioner in the dual role we have already discussed. The dual practitioner is less obviously responsible to the rest of his colleagues than is a senior teacher whose performance in the nature of his position, must command the attention of all his colleagues.

Failure is a misleading or inappropriate word to use in counselling: its use is almost a misnomer. Counselling cannot be said to fail in the sense that a scientific experiment, or a legal action or a mountain-climbing expedition fails. The goals of counselling are too imprecise for us to state categorically whether we have achieved them, i.e. succeeded – or not achieved them – failed. The human clients who comprise the raw material of the counsellors are too complex for the fail-success analogy to be used without the most careful reservations. Furthermore that intrinsic complexity is multiplied many times over by the relationships which any client has with people other than the counsellor – his peers, his parents and others – and which affect his behaviour in many ways outside the scope of this book. Beyond this the effects of a particular client's relationship with his counsellor may not emerge until long after the relationship has ended in the face-to-face sense. In the special case of Gubbins I had no information at all which told me precisely whether or not his counselling experience in school had any long-term effect upon him, however abortive it certainly seemed to be during the limited period of his school life. And even if we regard Gubbins as a counselling failure we still do not know why he was. Was it because he was an unwilling client because he was sent for, or an unco-operative one because he did not want to be counselled anyway? Yet even if either of these answers is true, again we must ask why? We can go on asking questions, although we can never know the answers, because the Gubbinses of this world pass beyond our influence, and can or will not tell us when they are under it. Thus failure is a dangerous word to use, unless its use prompts counsellors always to look upon past clients and experiences and ponder on their responsibility for the lack of success. Failure and success are also terms which we use to describe our own feelings, when it is the client's who, sooner or later or never, will decide whether our contributions as teacher-counsellors were positively beneficial or merely abortive. Moreover it is worth remembering here that our contribution will rarely, if ever, be malignant in the sense of positively driving a client further along the road of personal and social ill-health to which he was apparently committed when first we saw him. Failure too is a dangerous word because it introduces into a counsellor's thinking an implication of a need for standards of success and failure and of the speed with which he achieves them. Teacher-counsellors, still less senior teacher-counsellors, must not be motivated by a desire to achieve 'success' and avoid 'failure', or to take on clients who seem likely to be rewarding and reject those who are difficult. They are not teachers pushing people through examinations, seeking credit for success and offering excuses for failure. Anxieties about failure and success are to be avoided.

Thus, I use the word failure in the counselling context in a particular sense, especially applicable to the senior teacher-counsellor at one definable and taxing point of crisis. For while all teacher-counsellors have to operate, as we have already seen, within the general reticulum of school and parental relationships, senior teachers who counsel feel conscious of their special responsibility as leaders and setters of standards within that general reticulum. Whether this particular responsibility restricts the counselling potential of such senior staff or not, no counsellor can work in a social vacuum: he is always confined to some extent by society's conventions, and I doubt whether even clinical psychologists and psychiatrists can escape this restriction.

Thus, it seems to me that the definable point of crisis to which the term failure may become applicable is reached when he has to decide whether to use the full influence of

G

his positional authority as a senior teacher to deal with persistently recalcitrant characters in his school after counselling has seemed abortive. By such people I mean those who not only make themselves a nuisance in their own right, but disturb others as well, reducing a class or a school to chaos. For the non-counselling teacher this presents no problem. He asserts the force of his authority at the onset of trouble. He does not feel obliged to enquire why a particular student behaves badly. Readers may note here an emphasis on behaviour. Personally, I dislike the often-used distinction between work and conduct. The two are related, for good conduct and relationships lead to good work; but even if they did not, it is conduct in class and round the school which gives it the better tone and air of self-control. There is no need now to list in monotonous detail the endless varieties of overt bad social conduct with which teachers are thoroughly familiar. In any case we shall look at this in the next chapter.

For a counsellor, however, the question is much deeper and more complicated. We know that he is orientated to asking why a student behaves badly—in the generally accepted meaning of the last word. He can do no other, and not simply because of his greater compassionate sensitivity. The question 'Why?' for him is the start of understanding human behaviour. Objective scientific interest is here a necessary companion of his concern and sensitivity. None the less, despite these qualities in him, is there not a point at which he has to say in effect to his student-client, 'Thus far and no further. Stop!'? Must he, having reached this stage, not then call upon all the retributive powers which are available to a senior member of the staff? Must he then employ them to check a process of disruption by individuals or collectors of them, to destroy their influence in the interests of the whole school community? Can he then justify such action through his compassion for and interest in the whole spectrum of people in it?

These very real and searching questions are, of course, part and parcel of the general problem which confronts society as a whole. For the law has to balance the offenders' needs for rehabilitation against the protection to which ordinary decent people are entitled. The sentence of the court is retributive, even though it is intended to be rehabilitatory as well. There are those who feel that the urge to reform offenders has somewhat overwhelmed the need to protect society; that the equation of balance which the law and the penal system seek to solve is being manipulated to produce the wrong solutions with the wrong emphasis. Schools are a microcosm of society after all: they too have their equation to solve, and senior teacher-counsellors in particular have their problems with which to deal. For them the dilemma is ultimate, personal and almost alarming; it is between counselling and giving orders one way or another. They know well that to launch a punitive assault on a student by verbal or other forms of sanction may be to destroy the very ethos of a counsellor's work, perhaps his own integrity, and possibly the personality of the erstwhile client in front of him. If this seems to be rather theoretical, I plead the need to think carefully about the real situations which must in practice confront counsellors. If it appears rather dramatized I justify this by the need to present the dilemma as forcibly as I can.

Perhaps we can crystallize the problem into a clash between loyalties to school ethos on the one hand and counselling philosophy on the other. In seven or eight years of involvement in counselling situations in my own school – situations of varying degrees of seriousness – I have felt this clash to be a serious reality on very few occasions, certainly not more than half a dozen. The social-class sample approaches very closely that of the area from which the school draws its pupils, and about three-quarters of the latter have had no tradition in their families of education beyond the age of fourteen or fifteen. It is not therefore a particularly favoured sample in social distribution. When the clash of loyalties has occurred, however, it has been disturbing, bringing with it much heart-searching and analysis of motives behind the action I took because all the

clients involved in the clashes needed help, whether I was the
person who could give it or not.

Reflecting upon these few occasions, however, the students
concerned seem all to have fallen into a particular category.
All were highly self-indulgent and showed no response at all
to extensive personal interest in them and in their difficulties
of home and background. Sullenness and reluctance to communicate in any way were distinctive characteristics, although
they possessed widely different literacy and articulacy when
they did express themselves. Their basic and common philosophy
seemed to be 'I want, therefore I will take or do what I want,
as and when I want to'. They gave no hint of changing in these
respects, although this may have been merely a front to
dissuade me from counselling. Attention to careers needs, and
discussion about their futures, without reference to prospects of
intellectual success, sparked off no reaction. They were not
materially deprived in any sense although they may have been
neglected in other ways. They came from no single social class
or income group. None were stupid, indeed some had real
ability. In general terms they reminded me of groups of young
men whom I used to meet in a young prisoners' centre, especially in their reluctance to face themselves and their situations
as realities. All this justification, of course, could reflect two
things: first my own emotional need to excuse a failure to
break through to them; and second, a corollary of the first, an
indication that they really needed deeper and more expert
therapy than I or my colleagues could give. There is no available justification of the first, other than lack of time and
soundness of my own judgement; but it is fair to say of the
second that there are not enough therapists available to deal
with every young man and woman showing similar behavioural
characteristics, who is not responsive to a liberal and humane
regime, who displays sullen non-co-operation in counselling
coupled with continuous and developing open defiance in the
public glare of the class-room, who may even finish up in the
hands of the police for committing offences while still at school

and then glories in them, who is a bully and yet singularly lacking in responsibility and full of fear when anything goes wrong.

The real problem for the senior teacher-counsellor here is the admission of his own inability to break through to a young client who, after care and counselling, persists in trying, consciously or subconsciously, to destroy the community of which he and the counsellor are a part. He has to recognize the reality that in any community everyone has duties, rights and dignity as an individual. Just as society uses its law to provide freedom for the majority, and protection against the malignant influence and action of the few, so too must schools at some point evoke their system of control to defend their majorities of ordinarily decent, if mischievous and naughty, students. If counsellors in school are seen clearly to undermine this principle of the defence of ordinary decent folk, to tolerate without limit the destructive excesses of the sullen and disruptive few, it seems to me that they must bring themselves and their methods into disrepute if not into contempt or derision. The consequences of this are really serious because it reduces the benefits of this particular type of therapy for the many others who might and do respond. Here counsellors must also recognize their own limitations and need for help.

Let us return briefly to what we mean by failure. Schoolteachers are often rightly criticized for their very short-term view of this. They generally estimate it by considering students' attainments and attitude up to the time they leave school. Yet, all too often ordinarily naughty students in school turn into highly responsible and sensible young men and women years after they have cheerfully shaken the dust of school off their feet. My own headmaster forty years ago said that he judged his students by the sort of people they had become by the age of thirty, and his successor once observed that his school was a school for the fathers of gentlemen. Clichés these may be, but at least they state a long-term view of school success which contrasts violently with the immediate end-of-school-life judgements made by most teachers. Moreover, there are young people who have moved through all sorts of penal institutions ending in prison, but who have, as one young prisoner observed, 'in the end, grown up' finally into people indistinguishable from others who have had less unruly earlier lives. For the counsellor in school, then, to use his positional influence and authority against certain pupils in public, in support of colleagues and other people in the sehool, may amount in his own eyes to failure. This simply means that he has not yet seen those pupils' emergence into social wellbeing and personal peace which one human being feels is part of another's birth-right of health. He has not cured, in Jung's phrase, 'the illness which is the suffering that tortures us all'. Let us be careful here, however, and remember that this is different from seeking to impose mere conformity upon students. I have often asked my student clients to keep the fire of revolt in their hearts and minds, not to lose the capacity and will to criticize, to challenge and to change society and its values. This is altogether different from the self-centred and sullen moodiness, the cunning and hatred which characterizes those whose activities I have had to suppress, after apparently fruitless counselling. Of these it has, on occasion, been necessary to admit to colleagues that reserves of understanding, compassion and concern have run out. I had at that point to admit that I had failed in the limited sense in which I use it. It may be that in the future, long after they have left school, the youngsters about whom I felt this way would grow up as I know others had grown, into fine young people. But at this stage, at this point in time, this had not happened; the method, the approach, the attitude, the ethos in which a counsellor has so much faith, had proved at the time fruitless, perhaps inappropriate, certainly unacceptable. The clients had gone their own way, heading inevitably it seemed to social degradation or personal disaster, misusing their talents in unadulterated self-indulgence. Even this kind of uncertain failure is not easy to accept. For everyone, teachers and their students included, finds failure in examinations depressing, frustrating, disappointing, or disturbing. Work and effort seem pointless. For the senior teacher-counsellor, however, these self-indulgences are a luxury which cannot be afforded. He has to accept and live with his particular kind of failure. It is part of the job. This capability must go with the self-criticism and awareness of his own anxieties which are parts of the counsellor's occupational hazards. Indeed it may only be tolerable because of these last two qualities. He may if he wishes console himself with a variety of compensating thoughts on justifications: that he gave all the considerable care, patience, time and sympathy of which he was capable; that in the end he had to support the 'good' majority in his community against their assailants; that the latter rejected totally the hand he had held out so that the failure was not his after all. We can always excuse our own failings, but a counsellor has to live with them without excuses. He may be disappointed but this must not deter him from asking himself why he failed, or where he went wrong; if, on self-critical examination, he really feels he could have done no more, he has to live with that situation; yet he cannot afford self-satisfied complacency.

The situation is complicated even further by the fact I have already mentioned that every senior teacher in a school is the veritable subject of continuous scrutiny by his junior colleagues. His methods, success and failures are studied by all those who seek a model or example on which to base their own approaches and attitudes to the job. Will they condemn him for the failure of a counselling approach? Or support him for trying it with a difficult client? Will they doubt his integrity and accuse him of duplicity if he abandons it? Or praise him for his adaptability and ability to appraise a situation? Personally I regard this as irrelevant. Counsellors in the triple or any other role cannot work with their eye on the bystanders; and let there be no doubt about the latter's existence, for any school grapevine passes the word that Mr So-and-So talks 'off the record' with students, however private the meetings are. Counsellors must have some faith in themselves, however self-critical or dissatisfied with themselves they must be. They are not there to score successes and failures, if these are really estimable. They are there to deal with people as they find them and counsel them with all the resources at their command in the light of their needs and in the context of the community in which they are. In the last resort they are supported, or sometimes inspired, by an intuitive judgemental sixth sense which operates through no recognizable or logical process. It gives them a sharp perception of others' needs, of when to tolerate and listen in private, and when to act firmly and decisively in public. Having done this they need to accept the situation they have created themselves, to live with it, to recognize the anxieties it brings and to be aware that they are a manifestation of the sensitivity they bring to their work. Sometimes, by no means always, their decisive firmness, their ability to say 'Thus far and no further', evokes a respect which had not appeared before, effects a transformation and creates a self-discipline which had not been there before. Perhaps – we do not know – this is because the counselling role he plays touches somewhere in the hearts of many of his toughest clients a chord of fair-mindedness, sympathy and justice. I can think of three occasions on which a firm line, after several counselling sessions, has almost transformed a client.

When all is said and done, however, the senior teacher-counsellor's triple role is sustainable. Indeed it has to be sustainable because its practitioners are the teachers among whom are to be found the experience, the integrity, the insight, the judgement which are the hallmarks not only of the counsellor, but also of any art, profession or craft, of any vocation. They are the bearers of trust and responsibility, of power and leadership in the finest sense of the words.

This section of the book is a list of conflicting influences and forces, calculated on the face of things, as one colleague put it, to tear one's heart out. The tutor who supervised my marriage counselling at times noticed evidence of the stress it causes me, especially when other more transient troubles abound. Much of their stress is, however, bearable given support by discussion with other counsellors and with outside specialists. It can also be mitigated by discussion groups among interested, if not counselling, staff within the school. This not only relieves the counsellor's own tensions but enables him to explain why he does certain things, and keeps him in close touch with those whose eyes are upon his every act. For senior members of staff to move into counselling seems to me to be part of the slow revolution in current educational method, but they cannot undertake it without training and support. Moreover, not all of them have the right personalities; to determine this needs selection.

IV

Counselling and school authority

1 *Types of authority*

Authority is exerted in schools through the various controls
which teachers have over their pupils. This is the manner in
which all control over people is exerted – through other people.
Such control, however, is of two kinds which we can broadly
classify as positional and personal. By positional I mean control
which is effective because of the position which the teacher
exercising it holds, which in turn is based on professional
status, and the sanctions he can use to enforce it. It does not
matter necessarily what sort of person he is. The controlled
people in this case accede to it without any spontaneous sense
of their own participation or responsibility. Such control is imposed not elicited. Personal control is a different matter altogether; for a teacher it is effective because its foundation is the
view which his students take of him; because he is the sort of
person who is respected by his students, and whose ideas are
regarded as sensible and fair; he is such a person as to evoke
from his students a sense of their own responsibility and the
need to contribute to the control themselves. In this second
case, his status in a school hierarchy and the sanctions available
to enforce his authority are irrelevant and unnecessary; loyalty,
respect, even admiration and affection for him as a person lie
behind the effectiveness of the control he wields. Certain personality types may be associated with the two types of control.
Positional control seems more likely to be employed by those

who feel insecure and uncertain, who have not come to terms, and are not therefore at peace, with themselves, who are easily upset by the opinions and pressures contributed by others, whose own sense of values may be under stress, and for whom clear thinking may be difficult. Personal control is more likely to be exerted by those who feel secure in their own minds, who are at peace with themselves. They are thus not disturbed by the opinions and actions of other people, even though they may disagree with them; their own scale of values is secure not only in belief but in the demonstrable truth that they live by it without being sanctimonious: their thinking is clear and decisive.

To state the authority problem in this way obviously polarizes the two types totally. They are virtually diametrically opposed to one another. In practice, however, most control over students is a mixture of the two types. Young teachers, learning the arts of the job, and with their personal reputations yet to be made, have little else but positional control upon which to depend at the start of their careers. With the passing of time, the acquisition of experience, and the spread of their reputations, positional control matures into the personal sort. Yet, even with the completion of these processes of development there may be occasions on which positional control and its attendant sanctions are all that is left to use in difficult circumstances. We have already seen something of this problem when discussing the dual and triple roles. According to the nature of their personalities, which vary infinitely from one extreme to the other, most teachers employ a mixture of the two, according to the circumstances under which they find they have to exert authority and the people over whom they may have to exert it. Readers may notice in this categorization of control an interesting parallel between the two types of control and the distinction, which we have already discussed, between the attitude and the *modus operandi* of teachers on the one hand and counsellors on the other. The parallel is not I think, coincidental, neither is it fortuitous that just as there is a range of control technique between the two different forms we have mentioned, so there is a range of attitudes between that of the formal instruction teacher and the counsellor. The connection between the two series of gradations from one extreme to another in each case must, we might think, have considerable significance in the debate about the feasibility of teachers being counsellors as well. It also brings us face to face with yet another duality in the educational field – that of duality in control.

2 *Law and order*

Having made a distinction between two forms of control we must at the outset make yet another clear distinction between the normal concept and practice of civil law and order, which apply to schools as much as to any other branch of the civil population, and the special provisions which schools must, in their several ways, make for maintaining so-called order and discipline. The latter are generally thought to be necessary for the educational goals of the school to be achieved. We shall see in due course what these special provisions are. In the general civil statutory sense, destruction of property, vandalism, riotous assembly, commotion and breaches of the peace, especially those resulting in damage to the person, are as unwelcome and unlawful in schools as they are elsewhere. In practice it is true that school staffs prefer to handle civil disturbances and misdemeanours within their walls for themselves. The police, however, can be called in to restore law and order in a school or to protect teachers who may be threatened in any way by students in the school, if a situation becomes so violent as to be beyond the capacity of the head and his staff to control it on their own. It is certainly a rare occurrence in this country for this to be done, but there are precedents for it in the United States. Whether such police action restores sensible relationships between staff and students is another matter. It seems much more likely only to be a temporary palliative intended to restore some degree of order as a precondition necessary for establishing proper relationships. Those responsible in recent years for the conduct of higher educational institutions have been reluctant to involve the police in controlling disturbances by students. This hesitancy to invite the aid of law enforcement agencies is presumably due to fears that to do so might inflict permanent damage upon the network of relationships in the establishment concerned.

In discussing the effect of any new education activity such as counselling, upon the working of authority and discipline in a school, we must be very clear that we are confining our thoughts to the special provisions which apply to schools. If, as we have seen, the civil concepts of law and order apply to schools as much as to any other part of the community then in schools we are concerned about something rather different from civil public disorders. We are not thinking of the prospect of gangs of children wandering wild, doing endless damage and endangering the persons and property of staffs, although the existence or threat of such unlawful activities in rather rare cases is real enough. There are machinery and agencies for dealing with these situations; and heads and staffs should not, for example, turn themselves into full-time detectives to tackle persistent theft, when there are experts who are better qualified to do this kind of work. It is, however, for them to decide what seems reasonable in any given situation and to invoke the aid of normal civil law enforcement agencies to suppress unlawful activities. This would not necessarily eliminate the root cause of the trouble. This latter may lie, for example, in inadequate staffing ratios which make it impossible for a school to divide into smaller groups large numbers of tough, anti-social, deprived, inadequate, near-delinquent or delinquent groups so that they can be more easily handled and given more direct personal attention than is possible with thirty or more young people. Such action gives them a sense of personal value, and is recognized in special schools and other related institutions as a means of educating such people with more care and effectiveness than is otherwise possible. It is a major, if costly weapon in the hands of education authorities. That they do not always deal with it in this way is a matter of great social concern which is outside the scope of this book. In parenthesis it is interesting to speculate whether the cost of such action would not be offset by a reduction in the numbers of those who later in life turn to crime and become a weighty financial burden upon society.

Thus, when we turn our attention to school control or discipline, we accept that school authority should in general accept and aim at that level of civilized behaviour which is acceptable and recognizable as that of any other part of the civil population. It is strange to many adults who are not in first-hand communication with young people to be told direct that the latter as a whole accept this concept of law and order themselves. The generally civilized behaviour of the great bulk of young people is effectively obscured by the publicity given by the mass media, the press, radio, television, to teenage aberrations on the part of a minority of long-haired youths or skinheads, or those sporting whatever other style is fashionable among that particular generation at any given time, including conventional suiting. The general notion of peaceful order in society is not therefore rejected, even in these supposedly disturbed times, by the vast majority of young people. It is vital for us to realize this when we study the effect of counselling methods in schools upon school authority so that we do not wrongly relate it to law and order. Young people do not, in general, approve of mutually destructive gang fights any more than they relish the larger scale adult disturbances known as wars. They are moreover quick to point out the hypocrisy of a society which seeks to impose on them standards of peaceful living which society itself does not seem to apply to its own activities. It is fair to say, however, that they are concerned about how concepts of civil law and order are applied to them, why it is applied and by whom. They do not always approve of police action; yet when they are challenged to do so, or their co-operation is sought in doing so, they will respond sensibly and display a capacity to organize and maintain harmony in a school which is quite remarkable to people not acquainted with them personally, as those of us who have sought their co-operation will testify.

I have dealt with this problem of civil law and order at some length because it seems to me the threat, if not the existence, of actual breakdown of law and order lurks in the minds of some people who question the advisability of more relaxed relationships in schools. It underlies their unwillingness even to consider them as a possible means to healthier and more harmonious atmospheres in schools as a whole, quite apart from advantages to individual students. This obscures and distorts our thinking about the special provisions which schools must make so that they can discharge the various duties which society puts upon them, and teachers in schools threatened by disorder tend to regard counselling as pure theory. Each school makes its own rules and regulations. These are largely the outcome of decisions by the headmaster and his governors, whose position is analogous to those of a managing director and his board or perhaps to a chief constable and his police authority. In considering the validity and relevance of whatever rules they make and the relation between these and any new educational activity such as counselling we need to look at two problems. The first is what the goals of the school are, and the second is whether these goals have any educational value in the personal-moral or the intellectual-learning sense. It may be, for example, although we might think that this was rather outdated, that one goal was to secure total obedience to the school rules themselves, and that however the rules were made or however arbitrary they were, absolute obedience to them was intrinsically good for the students concerned because it engendered habits of living which would prove useful in adult life. Clearly the goals themselves and their value are closely related, and I propose to treat them together. One comment is, however, pertinent here, that in the last half-century education in these islands has neglected the goals of personal-moral and relational education in favour of the learning-intellectual sort. The former, however, in terms of the future needs of human society may be much more important for youngsters who are being educated at the present juncture in society's evolution. The learning-intellectual emphasis has led to the creation of particular systems of school authority, because it was thought these systems provided a stable environment in which the contemporary learning goals could be adequately achieved. Such systems tended to mirror the rigidity of formal learning. It is arguable that these same systems have been handed down to present-day schools even though the latters' goal has begun in recent years perceptibly to change, and that they now have little relevance to the newer goals of personal development and relational harmony. We can extend this line of thought further and say that the goal of most arbitrary systems of school authority is no more nor less than conformity to them, regardless of their educational or philosophical significance. Such conformity may in the ultimate analysis not withstand rational investigation, but in order to look at the relationship between counselling and systems of school authority we must try to break the latter down into its component elements and see what sense if any lies in them.

3 *The structure of school authority*

A school's regulations, which are the codified expression of its authority and the basis of its discipline, cover a multitude of activities including the following:

> times at which schools open and close each day; access to various parts of school estates; movement of students round the school; dress; homework; games; curricular choice; school reports; punishment methods.

There may be others, but a study of these will be sufficient for us to elicit whether school counselling will have any effect upon the structure of authority as it is displayed by school regulations.

a TIME, ACCESS AND MOVEMENT. Few aspects of school authority have a more rational basis than times of opening and closing, and movement round the school. Consequently fewer objections are probably raised about these matters than about others. Hours for opening and closing are determined by the need to make available sufficient time during the day to cover the needs of the school timetable. This is largely a function of curricular choice and arrangement with which we shall deal in a later section. Given the choice of subjects to be studied, which is made by the head and his staff in their capacity as specialist experts, the time availability is almost settled. Most parents and students are content to accept as sensible and fair whatever decisions are made in these areas of school life. Certain exceptions to this appear later.

Movement around school premises is determined by the need for commonsense safety and freedom from disturbance in corridors and passages and the need to safeguard the fabric of a school from the activities of minor vandals. In civic life we have rules for roads, escalators and lifts; at sea we have navigation rules; in factories we have safety regulations. Movement round schools fits into generally accepted patterns of ordinary civil conduct. Here again there are few objectors because the system in general seems rational.

When we come to access and egress, however, the situation is slightly different although rules may vary according to circumstances of different schools. Students are not allowed in the building before a certain time; if the school has grounds to it, students are forbidden to move about in certain parts of them; they may not be allowed out of school premises at lunchtime; they have to stay in school until it officially closes even when they have three free periods for private study at the end of their day's timetable. Is there a logic to this kind of regulation? If so what is it? Are we influenced by considerations of student safety in not letting them out at lunchtime or at the end of their working day? If so, is this a valid consideration for students who are sixteen years of age or older? We might agree that it was a fair regulation for eleven- or twelve-year-olds or younger. Indeed there is a legal basis for restricting the freedom of very young children to leave school at unusual times in a House of Lords decision in Ward *v* Hampshire County Council (1969). In this case a five-year-old child was allowed to leave school five minutes before the normal time of school closure. It was customary for the mother to meet the child at the normal time, but in this instance the child set off home on her own without waiting for her mother and was injured by a lorry while crossing a busy road. The mother had not been informed of the fact that the child was leaving early. This decision applies to the particular facts of the individual case, and it is perhaps doubtful whether a similar decision would have been given in the plaintiff's favour if the pupil concerned had been a young man of sixteen or more who would be thought to be perfectly capable of crossing the road in safety whether he left school early or not. In this case five minutes would be a triviality, although it was a significant period for the five-year-old.

It is not my function in these pages to decide the age at which such a period as five minutes or any other length of time ceases to be crucial or to arbitrate upon the age at which a student becomes capable of finding his or her own way home. The point of the matter is that access and egress for young adults must be much more a function of their own sense of responsibility than one of arbitrary rules which are framed with the safety of young children and the legal responsibility of the school in mind. Because counselling is much more an activity in which these older students are involved, its connection with this particular manifestation of school authority becomes important. Why then do we make rules about access and egress? Do we really fear that students are likely to kill themselves if they go home as soon as their official teaching periods are ended, as they would do in further education establishments? Do we believe that students of fifteen years of age or more will necessarily knock the school furniture

about if they are allowed into school, unsupervised, before the
bell rings at official opening times? Or is this done to prevent
theft from other students' desks or rooms? And if this is the
reason what sort of school organization can involve the students
themselves to prevent these costly, disturbing and anti-social
activities? How far can the sense of responsibility of the majority
of students be harnessed to counter the irresponsibility of the
minority? It is certainly true that some schools involve their
senior students more and more in day-to-day management
problems of this kind. They institute graded systems of privilege
and duties for older students, and have school councils in
which staff and students work as management partners. It is
equally true, however, that many schools have no such organizations, still less the will to establish them in order to give
greater freedom and responsibility to students as they grow
older. After all, this is part of preparing them for managing
their own lives when they leave the relative shelter of school.
Why do schools not do this?

It is not my purpose in this book to provide answers to these
and cognate queries about day-to-day school management.
These are matters for which heads, staffs and governors are
responsible and about which they must take the appropriate
decisions. They are, however, questions which arise in the
quiet of a counselling room. They are part of the irritation
and exasperation which emerge when counselling students of
sixteen and older who are smarting, *inter alia*, at the affront
to what they regard as their dignity and responsibility implied
by enforced adherence to rules made, as they read them, for
eleven-year-olds. The growth of sixth forms enhances the force
of complaints about arbitrary regulations which do not appear
to be related to their age or needs. Where such rules still
remain in force, one current consequence is that they are flouted
by the sixteen-plus age group, because they are neither rational
nor enforceable. This, it seems to me, is inherently dangerous
because it tends to engender a general contempt for all school
regulations, which is then extended to the law in general

outside school. Thus it is important that school regulations, especially those affecting senior students must be seen to be rational and workable, not ridiculous and floutable.

It can be argued, of course, that discussion during counselling of rules which are silly is intrinsically unwise, and that their modification should be left in the hands of far-seeing adults if they are to be modified at all. This, however, does not relieve teachers who counsel of the burden of facing the questions about school rules and organization when these come out in counselling. Students will ask that if we cannot give rational answers to them, why do we adhere to the rules which provoke the questions? If students in counselling ask for justification of rules, we cannot forbid the questioning or evade an honest justification. If we are forbidding or evasive we undermine or destroy the whole counselling relationship, and effectively stifle in the client's mind any discussion of other issues which for him are more deeply personal or serious. Questions about school regulations may only be a test of the counsellor's good faith before moving on to the deeper problem which lies behind a particular client's approach to a counsellor. The answers which, I repeat, cannot be evaded often provoke from the client nothing more serious than reactions varying from 'That is fair enough' to 'What a lot of nonsense'. The matter more often than not ends there, simply because the counsellor has faced the questions openly and in good faith without ambiguity or duplicity.

Any counsellor working in partnership with his client is bound at one stage or another to ask himself whether he cannot extend the partnership beyond his client to include the senior school as a whole in a joint study of such questions. Whether this is a practical proposition in a given school or not, he asks this because his relationship with his client, in these respects at least, runs contrary in spirit to the very existence of the rules which his client queries. Beyond this his conversations may be interpreted by a given client as an incitement to disregarding the rules. He may indeed feel this is true himself. A counsellor, however, can make a contribution to the co-operative evolution of school rules on to a rational basis; for as part of the context in which he counsels, he can discuss with his clients the existence of a reality which includes rules which the client cannot immediately change and with which he has, therefore, for the time being to live and abide. He can help his client to understand this not only as part of developing self-control in a situation he cannot change but also as part of the client's contribution to the relationship with his counsellor. It is not, and this is true also of other aspects of school authority at which we shall shortly look, a counsellor's job to take up cudgels openly on behalf of a client who simply complains about a particular rule which he finds irritating at a given time. Teacher-counsellors may not be in a position to do so anyway unless they are senior staff members. They should be very wary of doing so even if they are senior staff members whose advice is influential, lest they expose their motives in counselling to suspicion and charges of bad faith. Despite these reservations, however, counselling in schools compels teacher-counsellors to think hard about the sense and relevance of rules about school organization, and to be cool and rational about criticism which they will undoubtedly receive. Having done so, they can then justifiably turn a client's attention to their own attitudes, so that they do not see counselling merely as a form of grumbling and complaint without examining themselves.

b DRESS. Regulations about school dress or uniform are a constant source of irritation and friction, and some educational pundits decry the idea of school uniform entirely. This does not, however, seem to be a major issue among youngsters who have gained admission to a new school at the age of eleven. Their parents sometimes find the cost and serviceability of uniforms a matter of some complaint, but it is unnecessary here to discuss at length the advantages which school uniform confers upon its wearers in terms of belonging to a community, pride and loyalty, and a kind of identification with other pupils

at this rather tender age. However, from the age of fourteen
or even a little earlier, the picture of blissful and enthusiastic
acceptance alters. Ties change, shirt colours alter from the
drab grey or white to a range of hues. Pullovers, instead of
grey become yellow, purple, bright green and whatever else
gives their wearers a feeling of self-assertiveness. Standard types
of shoe vanish and a plethora of assorted fashions takes their
place. Perhaps some of this sartorial rebellion represents a
wish to conform with a community other than the school – the
gang outside school. This can be dangerous, if it leads to
association with law-breakers in the civil sense. And this
peacock-like brilliance provokes reactions among school
authorities. Brightly coloured socks, even sombre-hued ones
with an unobtrusive pattern on them have been known to
make some pedagogues bristle with outraged fury. Yet perhaps
all this decoration is but a healthy sign of self-assertion and
growing independence which is perfectly normal at this stage in
life, or a demonstration of a wish to abide by the dictates of
adolescent fashion. More significantly it may be an objection to
drowning individuality in a sea of drab uniformity or to losing
identity, according to the character of the individual concerned.
Hair style is especially open to this kind of interpretation, and
like dress, it has rather less to do with the quality of the person
beneath the façade than a grumbling adult world often
believes. The same sort of observations can equally be made
about young ladies in school, whose opportunities for sartorial
display, elegance and good taste are possibly greater than those
open to young men. Yet some time ago it was amusing to hear
girls complain about schools which would not let them wear the
black stockings which their parents had bitterly resented
having to wear when they were at school. This merely exemplifies the relative triviality and transience of the matter. It
also blinds us to the possibility that young men and women
can be encouraged to develop good dress sense, to attire themselves becomingly, without the confining regulations of school
uniforms. They often wish merely to demonstrate their good

taste and responsibility through free choice, rather than through imposed rules, which are not necessarily based upon good taste, style or design anyway.

It is true of course that good taste and responsibility do not inevitably follow from the exercise of free choice: neither is there any objective evidence that it is an inevitable consequence of the rigid enforcement of school rules. I recall one fifteen-year-old character, who possessed real ability in academic terms alone, despite a rough exterior. He suddenly appeared in a rather gaudy outfit displaying almost as many colours as there are in the spectrum. Attention was drawn to these aberrations using such epithets as 'shocking' and 'disgraceful'. At the same time he became rather loud-mouthed, or so I was told, for I had not personally noticed any of these facts. Perhaps this is rather remiss of me, but all I observed was that he became so disorderly and unco-ordinated in my laboratory as to amount to a public danger. The coincidence of these three sets of phenomena was in fact part of a pattern of development, but this was not widely accepted as a legitimate excuse. However, I had a few consultations with him in private, asked him about the laboratory behaviour and used the opportunity to discuss both his dress and his loud volubility. Not surprisingly, he had not noticed these things himself. It transpired that he was spending much of his spare time with a group of boys a year or two older than himself outside school: he copied their outlandish clothes. There had been trouble at home about his association with them and his parents came into school. All told life seemed very difficult – in his eyes. People who nagged him at school did not help. Nothing more was done, and within two months he settled down again with the aid of a little counselling. The strange feature was that no one commented upon his return to sobriety in dress and manner. No one suggested that he should be complimented. I have often wondered why? Was his temporary aberration so heinous? Or are we teachers aware only of things which offend us?

The client's behaviour was not, I think, unrepresentative of those of his age whose personal backgrounds contain no tradition of education beyond fifteen years of age, and certainly no habits of conformity with the dress conventions of schools. Much in the education of these young people was and is totally foreign to their domestic setting. Without a background which supports them, and under the influence of a teenage culture which is more significant to them, he and others like him are bound to succumb at some stage in their development to that culture. To question the whole rationale of a system which tells them, *inter alia,* what to wear is thus perfectly natural. Other cases abound from time to time in the press. Students are banned from school because their socks are the wrong length or their hair too long, because their trousers are the wrong colour, or they wear traditional oriental dress.* The list is endless, and the children concerned have not been guilty of any breach of school regulations other than these. Parents, and particularly the teachers concerned, have put themselves in positions from which neither could retire gracefully. Children have been rejected, their very education interrupted for what seem to be very trivial reasons and with a maximum of publicity. Confrontations have occurred which could have been avoided and both teachers and parents have looked quite ridiculous. Yet it is simple enough to ask privately of some really untidy and scruffy, or even smart but non-conforming, characters, why they are so severely inattentive or unusual in their appearance. Sometimes some quite fascinating or alarming background information emerges from such quiet conversations, information which helps in understanding a given student's difficulties. What then do we seek to accomplish by these rigid regulations about dress and appearance?

Do we insist upon sartorial conformity because it is something which we experienced ourselves? Do we therefore feel that others should experience it too? Was it therapeutic to us? Or, do we insist upon it because it is a familiar facet of school authority easy to detect and enforce? Is breach of it to be taken as an

* *The Times:* 1st February, 1970.

assault upon our own personal security in the basically conflicting situation of the classroom? Or, is it a challenge to our own
tottering serenity in the face of change? Are we just frightened
that the 'rot will spread'? And if so, what do we mean by rot?
Is our control over students so frail that it depends upon the
ruthless enforcement of sartorial habits which are not always
relevant to smart appearance, and still less to the educational
enterprise upon which we are involved? I am asking questions
intended to make teachers think seriously about their motives
in imposing this particular form of school discipline, and about
the educational goals they aim at in such imposition. And if
readers feel that my questions are slanted let me quote by
way of contrast a group of sixth-form girls for whom school
uniform had been abolished. They said that this put them in
great difficulty, because they now had to choose what they were
going to wear each day. Moreover they now had little to change
into when their school day was over! They felt they wanted a
uniform which gave them some choice of style and pattern,
which was recognizably their school dress. Perhaps they wanted
the best of both worlds. On the other hand, perhaps this was a
not untypical reaction to a position of total freedom, the choices
involved in which were perhaps not only beyond their cash
resources, but also beyond their decision-making capability
each day of the school week. Whatever are the arguments for and
against uniform regulations, it is certainly a topic which turns
up in personal counselling and indeed in open class discussion.
In this relationship the counsellor has to answer the questions
already posed or others like them. He has to be honest and clear
about the sense of his own views on the matter. They may go
against the views of the authority of the school in which he
works.

  c HOMEWORK. Not so long ago the headmaster of a direct
grant school took the unusual decision to abolish compulsory
homework entirely. This caused quite a number of scholastic
eyebrows to be raised in surprise, until it was observed later
that his external examination results turned out to be better

after the abolition of homework than they were before. Obviously this was a very special case. Not every school has the sort of intake, student background and motivation which we might expect a direct grant school to enjoy. Neither does one swallow make a summer. Such courage is rare however: not everyone so firmly casts away traditional practices and habits and challenges in so doing the very basis of our insistence upon them. I once worked in a non-academic secondary school in which homework was disregarded for the first three and a half years of school life. Programmes of home study were only suggested during the fourth year when certain students had indicated their intention of staying on voluntarily for a fifth year to take external examinations. The results of these were certainly no worse than those of schools whose students of comparable ability had done formal homework assiduously for the whole of their school life. Perhaps the important phrase here is 'staying on voluntarily' for this presupposes some sort of positive motivation in the students as well as direct interest and encouragement at home.

This is not the place to argue the merits or otherwise of homework. This has been done many times by all sorts of people in all sorts of places. It is not in dispute that students of all ages must be encouraged to do some work at home in their own time, if this is at all possible. We ought to remember, however, that for some students this is scarcely possible because of parental hostility or indifference, and lack of the privacy in which it must be done. This indifference is not particular to any social class to which students' parents belong. I know one parent who regarded his son's homework as a form of unpaid overtime which ought to be unnecessary if the teachers were doing their job properly; and another who felt that it interfered with the extensive social life and entertaining which was an essential part of his own occupation. In both cases the respective children frequently found themselves in difficulty at school because of the unco-operative attitude of their parents.

The real problem about homework is not setting it or

marking it, but getting it in, and what to do when a particular master's rules about it are disregarded. Vast quantities of time and energy, leading to frustration, anger and exhaustion, are expended in enforcement of homework rules, often without any success in the end. We may well pause and wonder whether it is really worth making this particular effort. Apart from the damage to the teacher's morale, the effect of the necessary nagging upon the relationships between staff and students may be damaging to the latter's long-term performance. One teacher of my acquaintance openly admitted that on one occasion he made a prodigious effort to force his sixteen- and seventeen-year-old students to hand their work in on time. The only result was a deterioration in the atmosphere of the classes in which he taught them. He degenerated in their eyes into an authoritarian figure, and a relationship he had built up with care and concern over three years was destroyed in two weeks. The possible effects of this troubled him more than the essays. He said he would never do it again. Indeed he wondered why he had done it on this occasion, for, in looking back, his examination results and long-term student success after leaving school bore no relation at all to the amount of formal homework his earlier students had done. In academic terms alone his students' results were exemplified by a chap who entered a sixth-form career with a bad failure in his favourite subject but finished up by being top of his year at university in that subject.

To dissolve the argument further, if teachers do succeed in getting their essays, maps and calculations in on time, they are often exasperated by the poor quality and general superficiality of the work so presented. Let us here remind ourselves that we are thinking especially of adolescents fourteen and more years old, in whose personalities the stirrings of personal responsibility and self-assertion are beginning to appear. The key to success with these people nowadays lies not in peremptory orders, which often seem to them to have no basis of reason, but in motivation; not in enforced obedience to scholastic habit, but in an appeal to pride in their work, their self-interest and growing responsibility. They are being educated in our present social climate not simply to pass examinations either inside the school or outside it, but to live independently in the rough world after they leave its shelter; not to live by a rote imposed by adults, but to learn how to exercise initiative on their own accounts. And even if students have to prepare for examinations, as most of them have to at one stage of their lives or another, is it not better for them to be given guidance, suggestions and ideas for study instead of conveyor-belt production of time-honoured or textbook-recommended exercises which may appear to be and often are irrelevant for their needs?

There is another side to the homework problem however, quite apart from its nature or relevance. Whether it is enforced or whether it is quite voluntary an element of courtesy enters into its presentation and marking. Of course it is polite to hand it in at a time which the teachers concerned find convenient, not just at any old time which happens to occur to the student who presents it. This is a sensible form of social education anyway and easily disposed of by a few courteous words of explanation and discussion. There is no difficulty here. But if work is simply never handed in courtesy does not enter into the matter. Why then do teachers habitually work themselves into a fever about this? Do they regard it simply as personally insulting? If so, why? Many of them complain in this way about students' absolute refusal to hand work in. Are they offended because the student is really saying 'I know better how to organize my work than you do'? Is this a fair comment, or do we feel that no student in school can possibly know how to organize his studying? Do we believe that we must know better because *our* teachers years ago knew better than we did? Is it professionally galling to realize that these young people may in fact be better at organizing their affairs than we were at their age? Again, if so, why should we feel so strongly about it? Why should teachers fail to realize that the class or group before them consists of discrete individuals each with a different attitude, cast of mind and method of working? Do we understand that some of them may not yet have reached the stage of being able to organize themselves and may have to undergo the therapy of failure before coming to terms with their own weaknesses and limitations and thus realizing the wisdom in adult guidance? I can recall a number of students whose capabilities seemed to offer promise of high success in their futures, but at the first sitting of their examinations failed miserably. This and this alone was sufficient to make them realize through their own bitter experience what was required from them in terms of disciplined study and well-managed and dedicated effort. Teachers, rightly, have a concern to give students the benefit of their own experience because their sensitivity drives them to prevent young people being hurt and shaken by failure. Yet, can we really, in this day and age, put old heads on young shoulders? Are we in fact right to prevent them from being, as we think, hurt by experiences which we know will come to them instead of letting them sometimes learn the hard way? Perhaps we shelter them over-much – or try to do so – and unwisely.

There is another aspect of the homework problem which turns up from time to time. Are teachers frightened that parents will complain that their children are not being driven hard enough? On the other hand there is a vaguely comic side to meeting within an hour or two one parent who complains in these terms, and another who is concerned about the great length of time his child is spending on homework, at the same age as the first. Are teachers not prepared as professionals in their job – let us use the word *experts* quite honestly – to advise and reassure over-anxious or over-ambitious parents? It takes a certain amount of cool professionalism to speak calmly but firmly to a parent who says that he expects his child to be driven hard to become a doctor or sent into apprenticeship when, at the time the comments are made, his teachers think that these are very unlikely and inappropriate possibilities. At this stage, perhaps it is the parents who need counselling and asked 'on what basis are these expectations based'? How much does the parent know about the requirements of the medical profession or the apprenticeship. Is the one just a piece of latent occupational snobbery, and the other a wish to continue a family tradition, all against the wishes and capabilities of the youngster concerned? Last of all, do teachers turn away from analysing their reasons for insisting upon homework simply because it was a charade which they had to undergo when they were young and therefore expect modern youngsters to bear with it, as a kind of compensatory sadism?

All these questions come to a counsellor's attention when the floodgates of resentment about school are opened by his clients. What is he to say? How is he to answer these questions about this particular facet of school authority without seeming to undermine the status of his colleagues and the school regime as a whole? The teacher who is outraged by a sixteen-year-old's refusal to hand work in presents a counsellor with a real problem. However, the teacher-counsellor's influence can be effective even in this matter because he can understand his teaching colleague's feelings as well as his client's attitude and reasons, and so begin to bring them closer to one another: moreover if he is a senior man also, he can offer to his colleague the benefit of his experience and the authority which accompanies this. Practitioners in the dual or triple role are well placed to resolve rather than exacerbate it.

d GAMES. Physical activities do not appeal to everyone, but the traditional clichés about team spirit still persist even in the public sector of education. We can make a convenient distinction here between physical education and games. The former is a useful adjunct to the total health of any human being, excluding from this discussion students who are unfit and therefore transgress no school regulation. They may feel resentful that they are unfit, but that is another matter altogether. For the ordinary pupil physical education develops co-ordination and a general feeling of wellbeing. Lack of specific aptitudes like ball sense do not detract from its benefits.

Games are another matter entirely. Some students are

demonstrably incompetent at tennis, football, rugby, cricket, hockey or whatever other game adds to a given school's reputation. They actually look and feel ridiculous; they often incur derision from colleagues and condemnation from teachers for their total lack of skill. Such derision and condemnation may adversely affect their general behaviour and development. Moreover, games require kit, which is expensive. Some schools cater for their students by providing a wide range of games including plain running and making arrangements for golf, badminton and other sports. This gives everyone the widest possible opportunity. Even with such extensive provision there are always characters ranging from the bookish intellectual for whom physical activity is the very epitome of human degradation, to the wholly lazy character who cannot bring himself to any physical exertion at all. Others are simply frightened of being hurt in any way. Disregarding the professional zeal of physical education staff, who exude the same sort of dedication to their subject as do other specialists, why do schools insist upon compulsory games? They may be therapeutic for youngsters in the early stage of secondary education, but the growing self-consciousness of the adolescent sometimes makes him rather resentful. There are also those with unusual problems such as a reluctance to take their clothes off in the changing-room or to have a shower. This may be a symptom of emerging sexual consciousness which will pass in due course, or it may indicate some odd parental ideas about the human body; both these, and other reasons for this attitude, are matters for concern about the general mental and social health of the youngster concerned, if they persist for long. Such attitudes lie behind a reluctance to take part in physical education as well as games. They may indicate a need for specialist treatment.

We can ask here the same kind of questions about compulsory games as we have posed about homework, dress and access. The answers also present a counsellor with the same kind of dilemmas as the earlier ones did. There are additional questions however. How far are compulsory games a vital part of a school's public image? Is the price paid for the public image, in terms of student resentment, worth the gain to the whole community? Is corporate loyalty enhanced by compulsory games or is it in fact reduced? Is the ethos of 'team spirit' a myth? Here a counsellor who is faced with this kind of question has to know his own mind honestly and be prepared to justify it in the privacy of counselling. But the fact that he listens may be interpreted as undermining the status and reputation of those to whom compulsory games are important. And if they loom large in the hierarchy of school activities and achievements this interpretation becomes more likely.

e CURRICULAR CHOICE. Earlier in this chapter we saw that given the range of subjects which a school offers in its curriculum the times of opening and closing are virtually self-evident and present no problems. The exceptions to this indication of frictionless wellbeing, however, lie in the choice of subjects presented to a student at some stage in his school life. The total number of available subjects is such that it is simply impossible, in terms of time available, for every student to study every subject. This is quite apart from the educational desirability or the student's capacity to do so. Every school provides its own particular solution to this general conundrum, and no one school's solution ever satisfies every one of its students or their parents. All sorts of permutations and combinations of subjects are used to deal with this problem, but the general principle is that the total number of subjects which a given student studies is representative of all the subjects available; the trouble is the actual selection. If the school offers chemistry or art, to be sure, someone will turn up who wants to do both. If it offers any three out of biology, technical drawing, geography, history and German, there is bound to be someone who wants to read all of these and drop one of the compulsory subjects which is part of his school's curriculum.

The particular framework within which subject choice is possible is part of the school's whole authority structure. It will appear to be arbitrarily inconvenient, even stupid, to any

students and parents who are dissatisfied with the given organization. Perhaps for this reason the long courses for counsellors
which are provided by various universities pay much attention
to curriculum construction and choice, and some specialist
school counsellors include curricular advice among their
various functions. It happens too that this choice is often made
at the age of thirteen and upwards, at the very time when the
perfectly normal feelings of individuality and self-assertion are
beginning to make themselves felt in the students, and any
imposed choice arouses a special kind of resentment, to a varying degree, because of the particular age at which it is necessary.

Clearly there are administrative reasons for the necessity
to make choices. There is little argument about that. The rather
chilling question however is, 'Why these particular choices'?
Why not others? Whether a counsellor is an expert in curricular advice himself is less significant and relevant than his ability
to accept, as students have to, the management decisions which
have been made about the subject alternatives and to understand that they may not necessarily be the ones he would have
made had he been responsible for making them. As a teacher he
may well have to abide by decisions which he does not like.
They may even relegate his own subject to a very minor position
or at least to a position of less eminence and importance than
he thinks it justifies. When therefore he listens to complaints
about the system of subject alternatives he has to have come to
terms with the system himself and understand the reasons for
it. To be sure, the questions he will have to answer are probably
less searching than those he has to deal with under the sections
of authority with which we have already dealt, and to this
extent he will be under less stress, and less open to a charge of
undermining school authority. This does not deprive him,
however, of the need to be at peace with a situation with which
he does not necessarily agree. If he can demonstrate this to
those among his clients who raise the problem of curriculum
content he is more than halfway to helping them also to come

I

to terms with a situation about which they find nothing can be done, at least not immediately.

f REPORTS AND EXAMINATIONS. School reports and examinations are still great pillars of educational authority. Whether reports have any intrinsic value is open to question. None the less, parents expect them and most staffs do their best with them, although there is a surprising variation about the thoroughness and sensitivity with which they are written. The crucial feature of school reports is that they are, or should be, a document which is privy to parents and school only. They may lose any value they may possess if they are regarded as documents suitable for display to potential employers. Students complain about adverse reports because they say that a single bad comment will damn them for good. Their advantage is that they are a rough-and-ready documentary record of a student's progress or lack of it, and because they are written they have a certain advantage over the more useful close personal discussion and consultation with parents about their offspring's development. The chief complaint which is made about them is that they tend to be critical rather than complimentary. Why is this so? Why do we, as teachers, forget to be helpful and constructive? Are we still justified in writing them? Is this because we have been victims of the same system ourselves? On the other hand, reports of some sort will probably follow every student in a school through his life, and perhaps they should not be over concerned at the special importance attached to school reports. Counselling can assist them to understand this.

Internal examinations are the partners of reports. Their planning and organization are almost a religious ritual in some schools, such is the importance attached to them. Like external and university examinations they have collected their quota of criticism in recent years. Yet they are part of the framework of authority, for by their results people are prompted, relegated, chastised and corrected, and their long-term futures may be still affected by a single mark. Reports are often based

upon them, and parents make judgements about the progress
or otherwise of their offspring in the light of examination marks.
To crown all, prizes are awarded on their results. Perhaps
their only real values are two: first they have some appearance
of being objective in the sense that they are not wholly affected
by teachers' prejudice as day-to-day impressions might well be.
After all, teachers do 'take likings' for some students, and dislikes to others, which may significantly, if subconsciously, affect
their assessments of the work they do. Secondly, internal
examinations do give students some training practice in
preparation for the external and professional examinations which
may well dog them for a large part of their lives. Whether
it is merely fashionable to have them or not, examinations
are certainly criticized by students in private discussion, and
put yet another strain upon a counsellor's resources. In listening to this his position vis-à-vis the general authority of the
school is again challenged. The rigid attitudes of colleagues
may also be called into question, and their apparent dedication to examination results ridiculed, especially by the growing
number of students who are staying voluntarily into fifth and
sixth forms with no intention of following traditional and formal
academic careers.

    g THE RATIONALE OF SCHOOL AUTHORITY. So far we
have looked briefly at certain practical aspects of school
authority as it is demonstrated by school rules which regulate
the conduct and work of students regardless of their age. Let
me emphasize at this stage that I am not advocating the total
abolition of school uniform and rules about appearance, of
set homework, of limited curricular choice, of obligatory
physical activities, or strictly controlled access to school by
students, or of any other convention which is thought by a
school and its management to be right and proper. Neither
am I advocating their retention in the form they are at any
particular point in the history of any given school. I am raising
a more fundamental question, namely: why do we impose the
rules, insist upon orders being obeyed, or instructions being

carried out? What is their educational value, in its widest connotation of developing a student's whole personality and his sense of individual and social responsibility? Does, in the event, breach of these rules or customs, necessarily and inevitably constitute or lead to a breach of law and order, or a partial or total destruction of school control and ethos? What is the effect, in these educational terms, upon the development of a given student, of the enforcing sanctions which lurk behind such rules and regulations? Does the enforcement system invoke fear as an educative agent? Is it effective anyway? Or desirable? And perhaps the most important question is whether the disturbance entailed in conventional relations between students and staff is greater or less than that which might be occasioned by abandoning rigid systems of control, assuming that an abandonment would necessarily be followed by any increase in disturbance? Many teachers seem to believe that to raise the questions in counselling will be followed by disruption of school order. Let us therefore examine the background and significance of these negotiations so that we may better anticipate the effect of counselling upon them.

School authority and control seem on the face of things to be an irrational hotch-potch of bits and pieces, apparently unconnected with one another. But these components have certain features in common. The first of these is a historical background. Those who can think back to schools in the 1920's and '30's will remember the rigidity of school rules then. It is no exaggeration to say that in a great many schools nothing has changed much since. Indeed, I have already commented upon the fact that young teachers in their twenties still try to enforce the kind of customs and rules which they experienced only five or six years ago. Moreover, adults who are not in teaching often recount tales of their schooldays, their escapades and punishments with a peculiar mixture of relish and regret. They rather imply that much of the formal discipline was rather fatuous and had greater propensity for encouraging mischief than for sensible personal development towards responsibility.

It does not, therefore, follow that a historical origin confers upon a particular system an intrinsic merit. Indeed business men are quick to point out the need for change and the ruthless casting out of outworn methods in the interests of efficiency and effectiveness. And when we speak of historical origin, what we are really saying is that there is no logical or experimental basis for the particular method of educating young men and women which we are examining. That method simply appeared out of the mists of history without previous thought about its relevance to the aims which it was intended to achieve. I am therefore suggesting that when we speak about school authority we ought to look very carefully at what lies behind the way in which we traditionally sustain it. We should consider what rationality supports its retention; if there appears to be none we should seek for it and if we cannot find any, then we should introduce a system which is rational in the sense of meeting current human and social needs, and makes sense to those controlled by it.

The second issue is that breaches of all rules which make up a school's total authority have to be supported by a punishment system. This involves lines, detention, beating, imposition, withdrawal of privileges – the latter assuming that there are any to withdraw. This topic has been recently much obscured by emotional argument over the limited problem of corporal punishment. Such an obfuscation of the whole control problem is unfortunate and not only prevents rational discussion of school discipline but also conceals the intense damage which can be done to a student by the kind of verbal indignities which schoolteachers still abundantly heap upon their students. None of these traditional punishment systems has any rational basis, unless we include historical origin in the category of sensible reasons. There is no research which proves their effectiveness. It is, of course, true that the ordinary civil law contains a substantial retributive element; but accompanying it there is also a rehabilitatory contribution which is notably lacking in most school systems of punishment, whether they consist of lines, detention, or caning. The rehabilitatory factor is now regarded by society as increasingly important; and beyond this, civil and criminal law is beginning to look much more carefully at causes of anti-social conduct as well as at rehabilitation and restitution. It seems to me that schools ought to mirror this trend in social thinking much more than they do. After all if they cannot look at causes and cures and restitution, who can?

The third common factor of the paraphernalia of school discipline is that it is a self-perpetuating system. By this I mean that the majority of schoolteachers have themselves, even in these enlightened days, been the products of schools in which such arbitrary and traditional systems existed. They therefore see no reason why such systems should not be perpetuated in the schools in which they teach, because they know no other way of doing things. This is what schools should be like in their view. This is something with which they are familiar. It contains no element of the unknown or the uncertain. *They* are secure in it, and this blinds them to the fact that today's children may find it neither secure, sensible nor relevant.

Historical origins, supporting sanctions and self-perpetuating systems constitute a formidable barrier to change. Anything which breaks through this barrier brings us into contact with the unfamiliar, the uncertain and the unknown. The barrier manifests itself as teacher-conservatism, and there are only two ways to achieve a breakthrough. The first is radically to alter the system of teacher training. This is far too great a subject for me to deal with in the scope of this book, although I hope it may make some small contribution to the debate. The second is for teachers on their own motivation to examine their attitudes towards school authority in the light of their own characters and their own view of the goals of education.

Let us put all this in summary form. To what extent do teachers regard breaches of school rules about dress, appearance homework, games and school access, as personal affronts to their own egos? How far do they rationalize a sense of personal insult at such breaches by invoking the aid of systems of punishment? Do we exercise control and support it by sanctions because it is educationally desirable, or because it bolsters our own self-esteem? To raise this problem in such blunt terms is perhaps to put the cat among the pigeons, and I do so simply because in discussing counselling methods with teachers in various parts of the country the conflict between counselling and authority has emerged as a critical issue. Too many teachers have responded to the initial challenge of the counselling approaches by angry expostulation about position and status, about undermining their authority. Some of them little realize how searing a light such objections cast upon their own personalities and attitudes to their social task. On being asked why they responded so sensitively, some of their protests degenerated into a state approaching incoherence, while others have admitted that they had never thought about the matter in these terms at all. In the response of this latter group there are signs of encouragement. For despite their admission that conventional systems of school rules were something they had experienced at school themselves, had been trained in at college and returned to when they started teaching, they became aware for the first time perhaps that there might be something amiss, and that other approaches might be sounder in every way. Up to this point in time they had had no contact with anything else. How, they asked, could they therefore be expected to cope with any other kind of working environment, such as the counselling approach? In this relationship would their values and standards not be remorselessly challenged by the unfettered arguments of minds ostensibly less informed and controlled than their own? Such a challenge with its departure from the normal controlled, disciplined and ordered class-room situation could, they felt, induce a sense of insecurity which might be damaging to their own personality.

In essence the problem comes down to a single question. Are the traditional imposed systems of school rules and the authority which they support a buttress to teachers' security rather than an educational need of the school population? Let me emphasize here the use of the words 'traditional imposed system'. I repeat that I am not in any sense advocating a system of no control, or advising on the desirability of chaos. For the present, I am simply inviting attention to the possibility of and justifications for the view that traditional enforcement of school discipline often satisfies teachers' rather than students' needs. .

4 *The effect of counselling*

The effect of counselling upon the hotch-potch of control mechanisms which constitutes school authority seems at first sight to be quite unpredictable. After all, we are enquiring about the impact of something – namely counselling – about which little is known upon something else – school authority – which is very confused. Even scientists who are acquainted with Heisenberg's Uncertainty Principle and the limitations it imposes on predictability will be forgiven if they recoil from thus considering a problem as complex as this. But the problem is presented by teachers and all manner of other educationists: if it is presented for our attention, this gives it some form of reality: and if it is real, even in this limited sense, we cannot avoid it. No counsellor can avoid a problem which is presented to him by his clients, and those who urge the claims of counselling upon school time and staff have to face the problems which that staff presents. They may of course reveal that the problem as it is presented is not the real problem at all, and that what is presented is actually a symptom of other underlying difficulties about which the doubters need reassurance of one kind or another. In my opinion the counselling versus school authority clash is a problem of this kind which is simply answered by the categorical statement that no such clash exists and that, therefore, counselling has no disruptive effect upon authority. To leave the matter there, however, is simply not good enough, for people believe it exists and that belief has to be eradicated. This can be done in two ways: first by looking at examples of experience, and second by further examining the working of counselling in schools.

a EXAMPLES. A fourteen-year-old alleged that a master had hit him, unlawfully, in front of the class. He was very angry and upset. He had been so upset that he had rushed out of the room muttering abuse, and now he did not know what to do. Should he go back to the next period he had with the teacher concerned? What was going to happen? What should he do? The question and the worry poured out. Perhaps he was just a silly boy. An old-fashioned caning might be thought by some to be appropriate. He cooled down after some fifteen or twenty minutes, but he had been so angry that he said he could not remember what had provoked the confrontation in the first instance. He went away with the promise of coming back the following day so that I could find out more about it. The need to do so was made more urgent because later that afternoon his mother appeared upon the scene; not in any aggressive sense, indeed quite the contrary, for she wanted to find out what had really happened because the lad had given her a story which was scarcely more coherent than the one he had given me.

If counsellors are to act as safety valves, listeners and lubricators, this sort of situation may be quite frequent. Trivial it may be, and some pedagogues would think scarcely worth the attention of highly qualified graduate experts in one subject or another. This is not the point of the matter for a situation has been presented and not even the boy knew what he wanted done – if indeed he wanted anything done. Moreover I did not yet know what the problem really was. Did an experienced schoolmaster really clout a boy in the full glare of the class? Whether he actually did so, or whether he did not, something was amiss. The question is what? The blow, real or imaginary, is a symptom not the problem. Briefly, it turned out that the teacher in the case had confronted four boys whose homework was consistently late or badly done, not in the factual sense, but in presentation. He had become rather cross. The client (who was one of the offending quartet) had muttered something objecting to what had been said to him, and bolted for the door. The master went to grab him. His hand and the boy's face had come into contact as the boy ducked. This comic tale is almost worthy of a television programme, but truth is often stranger and funnier than entertainment. The boy's workbook was really a mess, yet when he came back the following day he was much more concerned about how he was going to get back into the class, having run out of it. This was the problem from his point of view. From the master's point of view the problem was how he could get the boy to take a pride in his work, whether he was good at it or not. The two problems were connected, for if the lad could do something about the work, access to the class and the master's good graces was an easy matter. Another way of looking at this muddle was that the master's authority about work had to be maintained in such a way that the boy could return without fear of abuse or any kind of rejection. How then could both objects be achieved?

The lad himself provided an answer, when I asked him to show me his books, by volunteering to copy all the work up in a new one. No threats of punishment were made. The master concerned was agreeable to this, especially as the boy had to go and ask him for a new one privately. This enabled contact to be made in private without the rest of the class eagerly anticipating another explosion. The work was done, communication was restored, no one was punished, no one was resentful, and another bushfire of indiscipline died out without damage to anyone or anything.

We can take all sorts of views of this little incident. The rigid authoritarians would say that the boy should have been punished for idleness and misconduct right away, that to bother with his silliness was to exalt his importance above that of homework rules. But what good does this accomplish?

The point of the exercise is to restore a position from which *in the future* the boy can begin to work better, not to exact self-indulgent retribution for the teacher. One point must be clear however. This is an outline of what happened in *this* instance. It does not follow that this is the course to be followed with a similar case involving a *different* master and a *different* boy. I can say, of this case, that if the master had approached me first instead of the boy I should have treated the matter in the same sort of way, because this seemed to me to be appropriate to the personalities involved. Another point to be borne in mind is that teachers who want retribution before anything else do not consult counsellors. They get on with it themselves, although whether they solve the real problems for which they impose punishments summarily is a different question altogether. It is for them to answer this, not me. I can only guide if asked to do so. They have to come to the decision themselves.

A second example of a totally different kind came to my notice some years ago when a boy was detected using dinner tickets on which he printed his name over the name of another boy. This was brought to me as a purely disciplinary matter, and there is no doubt that authority was being flouted in every sense, that of civil law included. But why did he do this? All the signs were that it was not an expert job, certainly not the work of a youngster who was a habitual thief. He admitted the offence but was very reluctant to give any reason. This, I expected, might take some time, and arrangements were made to see him again. He promptly disappeared for three days. He obviously felt that I was going to punish him. A case can be made here for involving a teacher home-visitor, but the education welfare officer was asked to call at his home instead. It transpired that the boy was now playing truant. The mother was charming, but distressed. Father was out of work as the result of a merger which created redundancies and funds were running low. The boy was always given his dinner money, but finding some tickets loose in the playground he used these and spent the dinner money for that week on himself. He had not stolen the ones he used: he had simply not returned them to the owner. Restitution was duly made, but the activities of the welfare officer enabled the home to obtain certain concessions and grants, including free meals, to which they were, in their circumstances at the time, fully entitled. Everyone was happier and because the practical help was given by someone outside the school the parents did not feel that their pride was hurt. Here again mere punishment was simply inappropriate, given the facts as they were. With a different boy a different line of action might have been taken, but in this case relations between home and school were strengthened because someone wanted to find out why a hitherto quiet and sensible young man had done something quite out of character. Moreover his parents saw to it that he realized what he had done – and it is far better that they should do so.

Yet another instance of an assault upon the authority structure of a school was provided some years ago by a seventeen-year-old who was asked to write an essay, which he did not particularly want to write. Instead of the essay he turned in an elegant, articulate and logical condemnation of my request, all that it represented and what I represented to him. One fact is crucial about this case: I asked for the essay: he wrote a different one and handed it to me. No one else saw it, although I do not know whether he ever intimated to any of his friends that he had written as he did. As I did not know this, it did not bother me. This was a private matter between him and me alone, and as far as anyone else was concerned it had not happened. This particular fact in my view determined how the challenge should be handled. Other people with whom I have discussed the problem would not agree with my approach. Some thought that the document should simply have been torn up before his eyes, thus reducing him to his proper level of importance. Others have said that such a piece of impertinence was a matter for the head of the school, that he should have been told to leave the group of which he was a member, others again that he should not have been allowed to stay on at the school at all. His essay challenged school authority absolutely. Of that there was no question. But it was in private. The essay told me much about his feelings, and him. It was informative about me in some senses. In these respects it was potentially useful: information always is. Why had he written it? Why had he handed it in? Would he have handed it in to any other member of the staff? Was he simply testing my reactions, because I had invited the group of which he was a part to be totally frank in their discussions? Was he merely trying to show off? If the latter, why not say what he had written, in the presence of the whole group? These were the sorts of questions which came to my mind. These would help me to learn much more about him, I thought, and perhaps about those he represented. He could also learn more about me and the generation I represented as well as about himself. This learning was only possible if I accepted what he wrote and faced him with it in private to start with. Such learning is a part of counselling, as we have already seen.

He came to see me privately. He looked rather defensive and self-conscious as if he was expecting some severe verbal castigation. We sat down and I began, 'This is a most interesting piece of writing.' Prolonged silence! Then some signs of relief appeared, and a slight smile. The expected storm had not broken upon him, at least not for the moment. He seemed rather surprised. The details of the ensuing discussion are lengthy and do not matter anyway. The more relevant consideration is that from that first uncritical moment a relationship seemed to grow, which I think was probably mutually beneficial and which spread to the rest of his group in their periods with me. In retrospect, I feel that the others probably knew the general tenor of his essay and were curious to know my reaction. Yet they never abused that knowledge, assuming they had it. Instead a mutual confidence developed between us. Whether it helped to heal the scars of resentment at injustices which had befallen him earlier in his school career I do not know: at least it did not reopen them. The rest of his time at school was unmarred by any sort of misconduct.

b THE COUNSELLOR'S FUNCTION. Each of these examples illustrates an approach to a situation in which school authority was involved in one form or another. In each case no attempt was made to impose that authority, but serious effort was devoted to finding why it had been challenged. In these respects they are no different from many others in which homework or dress, times of access or compulsory games have been brought into question. The cases cited earlier in this book illustrate the same principles. Each of them, in their own way carried an implication of challenge to authority. In each of them the emphasis was placed on finding reasons for the behaviour which was called into question. Finding these, in some instances with the co-operation of parents, with or without the help of outside agencies, brought some amelioration of situations which could have grown into major confrontations between the student concerned and the school authority. This I believe is one part of a counsellor's job, but only a part. Even the boy quoted in the section dealing with the triple role modified his behaviour to some extent under the influence of counselling. To find out why things go wrong, why rules are persistently broken, to improve communication – all these are part of the role he has to play, if he is invited to participate in a given case by anyone already involved.

If a counsellor is not involved, either by the staff or the student concerned, he has no part to play at all. As far as he is concerned such episodes do not happen. It is not his business to go round a school deliberately looking for boys whom he thinks are being improperly treated, or teachers who are in difficulties of one kind or another. It is not his business to take sides in an argument; he is on occasion a sort of honest broker between two parties in dispute, although this particular, if quite inadequate, description of his role takes no account of his method or what he really aims to achieve. If students come to me with complaints beginning with 'Do you think it

is fair that . . . ?' they do not receive an answer to that question.
My reply is 'Why are you asking that question?' This helps
them to begin to think about the situation which is currently
on their minds. Staff who ask 'Don't you think that . . . ?'
receive similar treatment. Both are asking leading questions
and no counsellor worth his salt should think it is anything
other than a device to win him over to the point of view of the
questioner. If he is deceived into answering either question,
his good faith is immediately jeopardized; he is seen to be
gullible and impressionable, rather than clear-headed and
perceptive. If, as a result of a case or incident in which he
becomes involved, it seems plain to him that something is
amiss in the school organization and authority structure, it is
not his function immediately to bring about the changes which
to him seem necessary. If his position, e.g. as one fulfilling the
triple role, means that he is entitled and empowered to do
something, then he can do it with the normal courtesies and
consultation which he would employ anyway. But he cannot
interfere with or transgress rules which are not within his
province to alter. Counsellors should not, for example, tell
physical education experts how to run their gymnasia, or
instruct engineers in workshop safety simply because one
youth has complained to him about something which has
happened in either of these departments. For him to assume
that he is wiser than anyone else simply detracts from his
competence as a counsellor and destroys whatever confidence
his colleagues may have in his way of working.

To impose these limitations upon his influence and decisive-
ness is not, however, the same as saying he is powerless in a
given situation. One practically useful end he can accomplish
is to help his clients to look at ways of effecting change which
are sensible; to understand how they should go about making
suggestions; to point out the rights of others, including the
staff, in the school community. Sometimes it may in fact be
impossible for a suggested change to be carried out, because
it commands insufficient support among students or staff. And

if his clients are angry about this, he can then point out to them, that just as they have a point of view which they expect others to respect, so others have their opinions which are worthy of the same consideration and understanding.

In other words, counsellors are not primarily doers of things or achievers of material results in response to complaints and grumbles. Apart from anything else, to rush into swift action usually entails a breach of the privacy of counselling. They may listen, consult, suggest or urge: they can take the strain out of situations simply by listening to one aggrieved party or another, even probe and search for the causes of real or imagined difficulties. They can ask what are their clients' solutions to problems. They can advise senior staff and head-masters without saying what prompted their advice or giving names; they can mention that one problem or another might benefit from some attention. It has been suggested to me that this kind of activity reeks of underhandedness; and although I sometimes feel that this suggestion tells us something about the character of the people who have made it, the charge of underhandedness has to be rebutted by the recognizable good faith, openness and integrity of counsellors. Certainly little else will do. Here again we return to the essential importance of a counsellor's quality, rather than counselling expertise.

The last aspect of the counsellor's function in relation to authority is one which applies with equal force to his oper-ations in other fields of school life. This is that he must be able to tolerate a very limited degree of success or progress. He simply must not be hurt, offended or put out by having sug-gestions disregarded or advice rejected. Teachers working in tough schools with headmasters, whom they believe to be unsympathetic, sometimes complain that all this talk about counselling is so much theoretical nonsense, that their pupils expect to be caned for misdemeanours or called names, or whatever other form of crude control is necessary to maintain authority. How can they counsel under such conditions? Of course they are right. No one can counsel in the midst of total

chaos; or counsel competently in a thoroughly explosive
environment, or under a headmaster who does not believe in
it. But these critics seem to me to be trying to *do* too much:
they forget that their job (if they want to counsel) is to learn
to listen, to tolerate in private and to make relationships the
results of which they may never know. But the doubters want
visible or material results for their well-meant intentions and
efforts; they forget that this is not where a counsellor's *raison
d'être* is to be found, that there is no visible end-product to
most counselling. They have to live with this, and many
sensitive people find it thoroughly frustrating. If this frustration
becomes unbearable counselling is not for them. Moreover, I
remind any readers who may find themselves in this category
that counselling is not concerned with the sometimes grim
battles of class-room control, unless they are specifically asked
to intervene and guide. If they are so asked, then they may
begin to use their influence on trouble-makers and ring-leaders
and if necessary invoke the aid of outside agencies, including
the police, as I suggested at the beginning of this chapter.

I end with two examples which exemplify zero or limited
results. One concerned a boy from a very rough background
who was a liar, a petty thief and a regular truant. The school
consulted at one stage or another every agency which could
possibly help. In counselling, this young man was completely
two-faced and full of promises which were never fulfilled.
In this duplicity at least he was consistent. In no branch of
school life did he achieve anything, although his intelligence
was above average and his parents interested if ineffectual.
Every conceivable educational and social agency became
involved in his affairs, and the total of time, care and energy
devoted to him was by any standard enormous. He seemed to
be unable to communicate with anyone in any terms other
than the gratification of his whims, even within his own age
group. He isolated himself by his continued evasiveness and
dishonesty. In the end everyone concerned with and about him
admitted that their reserves of patience and compassion were

K

exhausted. Moreover he made such a thorough job of his waywardness that all fear of his encouraging others to copy him disappeared. He seemed at the time to be a classic failure, of social welfare and of counselling: his destiny seemed to lie with other human driftwood. Such failure is something with which anyone who involves himself in social welfare or counselling has to be prepared to live and to accept.

The second instance concerned a boy whose whole personality began to show signs of deterioration, if not disintegration. These were not the overt truculence, anti-social conduct, or delinquency which are easily noticed, but rather a subtle decline in work, and an impression of being completely at sea in life. He seemed dazed and withdrawn: normal considerate approaches brought no replies other than monosyllables and an apparent resentment about the enquiries. A succession of absence notes, which appeared to be valid, provided the clue when one observant teacher noticed that the appropriate absences coincided with him being seen doing various family jobs in the neighbourhood. Various welfare agencies became involved and through them it was established that his home background was in fact completely unstable, despite being materially adequate. The stress he had to endure at home was so great that it had affected every aspect of his life, and made him withdraw from any effort or activity in school. As far as his home was concerned the social agencies could achieve little, but in the final issue the young man resolved the matter himself. Once the situation became known in school through the good offices of agencies outside it, he came to a decision with the aid of a little counselling to leave home completely and settle himself in an organized and disciplined job. The alternative for him was probably a life of drifting unemployment if he had stayed. Here failure was not total; some resolution of his difficulties was accomplished, but in counselling terms it is a useful example of what was no more than limited achievement by the time he left. In the long term, the achievement may have been greater than was felt to be possible in the school at the time he went. At least he was helped to make his own mind up and take action on his own account, whether we as teachers would think this was recognizable as success or not.

Both these cases afford illustrations of conflict between a counsellor's clients and the school authority. Both counselling and the use of outside agencies gave some understanding of why the clients concerned were in such dire straits. This almost certainly helped to reduce any effect their defiance of school authority might have had upon other members of the school population. This last is always a matter about which teachers are anxious, perhaps unnecessarily so. If one boy gets away with something, it is thought that many others are likely to follow suit. But how often does this happen? In any event these particular cases were never resolved to anyone's real satisfaction. In some ways it may be said that such clients get away with it. But what satisfaction is to be gained simply by punishment in cases like these. What does it achieve? It was tried in both, anyway, before they came to my attention with no improvement in the respective situations. Both illustrate the need in some cases to live with what we might call failure.

What then is the effect of counselling in private upon school authority? We began the discussion by stating that the clash between them is illusory, but that this needed justification. The case extracts in this chapter and elsewhere are intended to show that teachers need to have no fear that counsellors will interfere with the day-to-day conduct of their own discipline in class. On the contrary the influence of the counsellor may in fact indirectly and imperceptibly assist in maintaining class control, provided that the teachers involved can accept his co-operation, as indeed most of them can or could if they had confidence in the personal and professional integrity of the counsellor concerned. None the less there still remains in this profession a considerable number of teachers at the secondary level who still view counselling activities with grave suspicion.

First, and briefly, let us dispose of the law and order issue raised by a minority of teachers who believe that counselling in private with anti-social students would only encourage them to extend their activities. We have mentioned this problem earlier. So far from helping such people, the argument runs, it would only make them feel that the freedom of expression which their lawlessness involves is right and proper: being free to express themselves as they wish to a counsellor in private is bound to stimulate their indiscipline so that they would feel at liberty to encourage others to break up classes, damage property and increase total disorder and assault other students in school to the point at which the rest of the staff would be helpless. The counsellor's acceptance of them would be their justification. 'If I can say what I like to him, I can do what I like to someone else': this is the thesis in a nutshell. I do not know of any evidence that the private therapy of the counselling type achieves this result. However, I should find it difficult to believe that any teacher-counsellor, with all the concern and sympathy and sensitivity which are his abiding qualities, would in fact in counselling encourage any client within the school to take part in, or lead others to take part in, lawless activity of this kind. Such a client must be disturbed in one way or another and ought to be referred if at all possible to another agency, be it the police liaison service, the probation service, a psychiatrist or any other appropriate agency or person, in *his own interests*. Treating cases of this kind is beyond the compass of school counsellors, although they can help in elucidating background information which could account for the client's conduct. Counsellors must be aware of their own limitations. The belief that they are universal trouble-shooters should not be encouraged. Indeed some of the enthusiasm for counselling and the implication of omniscience may be the very cause of the doubts about its usefulness not only in the special circumstances of the lawless client, but with the generality of clients as a whole.

The difficulty for some critics of course is where the line is to be drawn between helping young people in difficulties and appearing to encourage them to break the law. Perhaps the case of the boy who used dinner tickets belonging to someone else will help to indicate the borderline. This boy was detected, and checked, by the school. He was helped by the school and welfare service. No action was taken with law-enforcement agencies at that stage. It is fair to say, none the less, that had he repeated the offence we would have considered taking different action. The borderline in this instance is represented by the fact that he did not repeat it. Borderlines, however, vary, and this example is simply a guide line, not a rigid rule. Even in cases where a boy finds himself in court, a counsellor in school can often be extraordinarily helpful, first of all to the probation officer who has to make a report about him, and afterwards if he is put on probation. The supervising probation officer and counsellor can work together in confidence, without anyone else in the school knowing, to the probationer's benefit.

Now let us turn to the more immediate problem of the impact of counselling on the special authority structure of the school. To begin with, teachers who are worried about this one cannot evade the questions about that authority and its various components with which the first part of this chapter ended. These constantly recurred in the ensuing discussions, for in this day and age teachers have to accept that everything which they do, say and give instructions about in schools is, and will continue to be, challenged by youngsters, certainly those aged fifteen and more. They will attack rules whose origins are purely historical, and which seem to lack any form of rational justification. We all know perfectly well that these youngsters often argue from a basis of pure selfishness, of the 'I don't want to, therefore I won't' type. But the sceptics about counselling must remember this: while the young people ask, as I have asked in this chapter, what the basis of school authority is, why we have regulations about work and dress and all the other impedimenta of authority, so too does the counsellor ask his questioners why they take the view they do of these – to them – odious symbols of authority. He invites his clients, as I invite teachers, to look at situations in schools, and to consider not only their own views of whatever concerns them, but also to remember that there are other people who have different views. They, too, are surely entitled to know that their opinions are treated with the respect the client's claim for theirs, simply because they, like the clients, are people. My purpose in this book, in posing the questions I have posed to teachers, simple as the questions may be, is not to give the answers. This would be an impertinence. Rather is it to invite them to think about the questions and to think beyond them. In thinking beyond them they may next consider whether some of the things about which we make regulations are not rather irrational and that affairs in schools might run more smoothly if we substituted for them more rational systems of authority. Then perhaps everyone could get on with the business of education instead of worrying about designs on socks or why an eighteen-year-old who possesses adult legal status hands in essays late – if at all. The sceptics too must bear in mind that counsellors invite their clients to think about school uniforms and essays. Counsellors may even believe in the symbols of authority in their own minds but counsellors have to accept people as they are and feel – they do not necessarily agree with all they say. Whatever clients say they will be asked to justify or explain as part of the counselling process, which necessarily involves any client, even at the most elementary level, in thinking about his own weaknesses and self-indulgencies, as I have been asking teachers to do.

Thus the challenge which, on the face of things, counselling appears to offer to traditional authority systems is matched by a challenge to the clients themselves. We ought also to remember that counselling is a confidential experience, especially when it deals with personal and domestic difficulties. It has very rarely been my experience that a boy will go back to his classmates and recount in gleeful detail the burden of a very searching conversation, or series of questions. Youngsters keep their private lives to themselves. And if they did blurt out to another member of staff what they thought the counsellor had said, the teacher concerned can always consult his counselling colleague. This means that the youth concerned will experience another searching interview. The very nature of counselling is such that it has its own built-in safeguards against exploitation, not deliberately built-in but an intrinsic part of it, which cannot be removed.

A further safeguard is the view I have already expressed, if not in so many words, that counsellors are not busy-bodies looking for business or for faults in their colleagues. They are there to be consulted if people want their help. If students consult them, and complain about the methods of a teaching colleague, it is not, as I have tried to show, his business to rush to that colleague and tell him how to conduct his class or teach his subject. The counsellor's job is certainly to communicate and invite any colleague's co-operation in dealing with the particular student to the benefit of everyone. If teachers at this point feel that the last phrase means to their benefit alone, then they ought not to be in teaching at all; but even the most obdurately orthodox teachers will bend to some extent to meet the special needs of a young person who has desperate domestic difficulties for example. So much difficulty over school authority is caused by lack of information and communication. Counsellors can help enormously here, if their clients will let them, by giving colleagues some inkling of the latter's difficulties to masters into whose bad books they have fallen, even if he does not disclose details. So often have I heard this from teachers: 'If I had known or understood before what you have explained, I would have treated the youngster differently.'

Those sceptics whose implacable views are based upon continuous experience with hostile classes should pause and think. One or two members of their hostile classes might respond to counselling in private, and modify their reactions to school and adults in general through their acceptance by one person in particular. Even if this is impracticable or fails to elicit any response, they and their counselling colleagues have to accept and live with limited or zero success. Teachers generally have to do this anyway, but counsellors do not worry about it. Their temperament has to be such that they accept it without being complacent or easily satisfied with minimum effort on their part. Sceptics in this category seem to me to be often upset because they want to do something, or secure results quickly. All too often this is simply not possible. To be angry about this is to suggest the existence of anxieties within the person concerned, because what seems to be very slow progress does not satisfy their emotional needs, whether it helps the client or not. It is not the business of counsellors to tranquillize the emotional disturbances of their colleagues when they counsel their clients.

Counselling is about people and relationships. It is not really about rules, or supporting them, or subjects or teaching methods or discipline in class. Certainly clients start by criticizing them, but what they go away with is the germ of a relationship which more often than not is what they appeared to be seeking. Having found it, the initial or presenting problem generally vanishes. Often they cannot remember what originally prompted them to come. For the non-counselling teacher, for whom counselling may have a mystique I cannot remind them of this too forcibly or too often. Counselling is concerned with Martin Buber's 'I-thou' relationship, the feelings between people which confer worth upon them and value to human existence. As such it can have no challenge to formal authority in schools as a whole, or to individual teachers in their rooms.

Let us return to the point at which this chapter began. What we have been discussing is *positional* authority. This is the only kind of authority which many teachers recognize. In its absence they assume that there is no authority. We ought not to end this chapter without reminding ourselves that we started also with *personal* authority. This is the authority which counsellors possess: it is rooted in the sort of people they are and seem to be, in the way they conduct themselves and treat other people, in their hasteless calm and imperturbability, in their capacity to tolerate others without giving way to or agreeing with them. This needs no sanction to sustain it, be-

cause it is an authority which is attributed to them although
they do not seek it, rather than one which is imposed because
they need it. Thus when we say that counsellors neither possess
nor use authority, we are speaking of positional authority.
For this they substitute the personal authority which they
receive from others. This we may think is more durable and
significant than the other kind; because it is so, it can scarcely
be anything but a stabilizing not a disruptive influence.

Even so concern and suspicion is expressed in some quarters
that the counsellor's open-minded approach to his client in
school prevents him making any contribution at all to much-
needed moral education and may indeed vitiate it. In *Teachers
as Counsellors* I argued that counselling is a moral activity, and
that the educational problems of our time are moral and relational, not intellectual or vocational. The concern and suspicion
therefore need to be dispelled if counselling is to be accepted
as an aid to these goals.

Counsellors see their clients *as they are*. They accept and
understand feelings and opinions about moral issues as well
as about the relative trivialities of dress and homework. They
perceive that external appearance and examination perfor-
mances are not necessarily accurate indications of the personal
quality beneath the outward display. They believe that people
are intrinsically valuable. In so doing they establish communication with their clients, and once this is done the latter will
listen to them. The clients may not act upon what they hear
immediately or be instantly transformed by it, but they will
consider it instead of rejecting it out of hand, as they so often
reject moral preaching. It is interesting here to recall that the
Christian communions in England are deeply concerned about
their failure to communicate and some of them have begun to
use counselling methods in pastoral work. Quite recently I
also heard a police officer accept the criticisms and antagonisms
of young adults without rancour or resentment, answering
them with respect and calm. In turn their respect for his
calling and ideas was immensely enhanced by his example.

The counsellor's respect for his clients engenders their respect for others; his appreciation of their rights fosters their awareness of the rights of other people; his sense of duty to them stimulates their duties also; his awareness of their self-respect encourages them to see that others have self-respect too; his persistent courtesy, in the face of the most trying clients helps them to display courtesy to others. And when all else fails he can find for them better help than he can provide. All these facets of relations with other people are, many of us would think, the components of the healthy social life to which most moral training is directed. Even the slightest understanding of them starts a client on the road towards solving the moral problems of his whole life, as well as appreciating the intricacies and frequent absurdities of school authority. It may seem strange to some that we can possibly achieve moral goals in education by drawing upon the inner resources of the taught rather than by imposing the will of the teacher. It may well be the only method left to us. Whether they counsel with individuals or with groups, the total influence of counsellors upon their clients can scarcely accomplish less in terms of moral training than has been achieved in recent decades by traditional methods of indoctrination, even if that moral training is incidental.

V

Referral

1 *The meaning of referral*

This term is used to denote action by a counsellor which introduces into the relationship between him and his client the guidance or aid of another person. This action is dependent upon agreement by the client, and, where appropriate, by his or her parents. The person concerned may be involved in his or her own right, or as a representative of an organization; if the former he or she may work inside or outside the school. For the sake of clarity in this chapter, the term agency is used to include both organizations and individual persons.

The cases in which referral is appropriate can be conveniently classified into four groups according to the counsellor's view of the situations presented by his clients.

a. Cases in which the counsellor consults an agency for guidance and advice to support him, not with the immediate intention that the agency shall take the client over itself.

b. Cases in which the counsellor believes it would be in the client's best interests for the agency to take the client over, at least for some time, however short. This category of agency involvement could conceivably follow the first.

c. Cases in which a counsellor contacts an agency which can give material help to a client, to support him in giving a client better advice in response to the latter's request for help, than he has so far been able to give.

d. Cases in which the counsellor acts as an intermediary, in putting the client in direct contact with an agency which can give him practical help.

We should note in these categories two useful distinctions. First, the distinction between support to the counsellor himself, so that the client is aided through the counsellor and not directly by the agency; and direct guidance by an agency to the client, the counsellor being eliminated from the case at least for the time being. Secondly, the distinction between guidance and advice on the one hand, and material help and practical provision on the other.

2 *Managing referral*

Defining referral does not indicate how it is managed in practice. Fitting a counselling service into the day-to-day work of a school is a management problem itself; so too is operating a referral system which entails the establishment of links between the counselling service and outside agencies. Mr Victor Feather, General Secretary of the Trades Union Congress once wrote* that management is not a passive matter. It involves making decisions upon whatever evidence is available in relation to the aims in view. In the context of counselling and referral this is as true as it is in the context of industry and commerce. It means that deliberate and clear decisions must be made in a school about the following matters:

a. Who counsels and when
b. Who organizes referrals and when.

Decisions in the first category must be made by the head of a school in consultation with his prospective counsellors and panel of selectors. Decisions in the second category should properly be the responsibility of individual counsellors, such responsibility being delegated to them by the headmaster.

* *The Times*: 27th April, 1970, 'Workers' loyalty must be earned'.

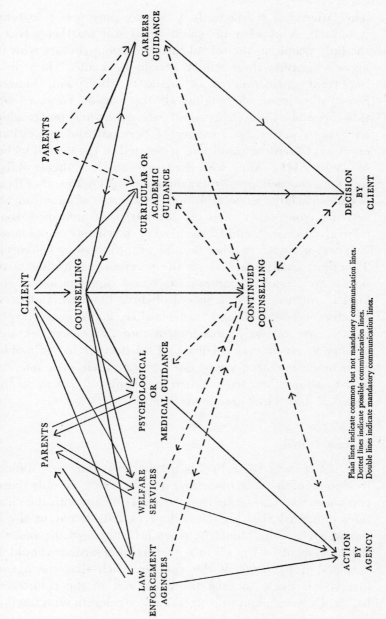

POSSIBLE RELATIONSHIPS BETWEEN COUNSELLING, SUPPORTING AGENCIES AND PARENTS

CARERS GUIDANCE

PARENTS

CURRICULAR OR ACADEMIC GUIDANCE

CLIENT

COUNSELLING

DECISION BY CLIENT

CONTINUED COUNSELLING

PSYCHOLOGICAL OR MEDICAL GUIDANCE

PARENTS

WELFARE SERVICES

LAW ENFORCEMENT AGENCIES

ACTION BY AGENCY

Plain lines indicate common but not mandatory communication lines.
Dotted lines indicate possible communication lines.
Double lines indicate mandatory communication lines.

The latter, less satisfactorily I believe, may prefer to retain it himself. A number of school heads still see themselves as the only people in the school through whom contact with the agencies outside their schools should be made. There is an important distinction to be made at this point, between heads who insist on making all the outside contacts, and those who like to be informed of external arrangements which have been made, as a matter of personal and professional courtesy. Given the conditions stipulated in the second section of Chapter III dealing with the triple role, it is almost obligatory for a counsellor to display this courtesy. On the other hand, of course, in large schools this may be a matter of some difficulty and if anyone other than the head is to be informed about referral action it should be the head of the client's school house, his year, or whatever other division of the school he belongs to. This must clearly depend on the precise organization of the particular school. Communication and organization of any kind is much easier in a school of three hundred students in which everyone, staff and students alike, knows everyone else, than in one of twelve hundred or more. However, we shall assume purely for convenience that the decision in a school has been made and that counsellors arrange their own referrals. Two questions then arise. 'When are clients referred to another agency?' and 'How are clients referred?'

3 *When to refer*

The first of these, the 'when' of the matter is extremely difficult to answer in anything but rather general terms, for only one or two conditions can be defined easily. To begin with the client must either ask that his counsellor seek outside aid, or else he should agree to it voluntarily when it is suggested. Beyond this the agreement of the client's parents or guardian should be obtained if the facts of the case are such that the agency involved is likely to take the client out of the counsellor's hands. Counsellors must support and co-operate with families, not replace them. Even those whose thinking is coloured by experience of inadequate, hopeless and criminal families must not assume that they have a kind of divine right to 'take over' such people. It is not for teacher-counsellors to decide whether a thoroughly hapless family is incompetent to manage its affairs. We are all jealous of our own privacy, even if it is the privacy to make a complete mess of our own lives, at least to the point at which the law is empowered to intervene. Then it is for the courts to decide what is to be done. That privacy must be respected. In practice families welcome help if they are really in difficulties or embarrassed, and are often ignorant of aid which is available to them if they ask for it, and unaware of the privacy which rightly surrounds the grant of it.

The circumspection with which a counsellor must approach a family is easy enough to understand if we all constantly remember this desire for privacy to work out our own salvations. It is much more difficult, however, for any counsellor to assess the point in counselling at which it is appropriate to seek guidance or help for himself or his client. We have already looked at the influence which our own anxieties have upon our handling of any case, and it is very easy to develop feelings of panic about our own ability to cope with a given situation. The boy mentioned in Chapter III, who came out of an examination in a state of severe stress, is a case in point. A client like this is in a kind of panic himself or approaching it. He cannot therefore gain any confidence from talking with an adult counsellor who merely responds to him by panicking himself, especially if the client's family are prone to similar anxiety states. Much of the therapy he requires has to come from someone who is not himself disturbed by the anxiety of others, but manages to live quite equably with it. Clients can gain confidence from the knowledge that other people experience or understand the same sort of feelings as they are beginning to think are unendurable. Counsellors themselves find confidence in discussing cases which worry them with other counsellors in private, and weighing with them the pros and cons of referral. While we should be sensitive to abnormality, we should not always jump to hasty conclusions about glassy stares, eyes with dilated pupils, highly strung or variable behaviour, acute pallor and haggard features, and whatever else is symptomatic of drug or other disturbances. The majority of cases before us are not social misfits or victims of whatever current aberration rightly concerns all of us a great deal. Social maladies receive much publicity but this should not divert counsellors from the central purpose of their activity, which is to make a relationship with their clients so that the latter feel secure, the stress in which they are or believe themselves to be is reduced and they begin to feel better able to cope themselves with their situation. If a counsellor feels this relationship is strong enough for him to suggest involving someone else, or he needs support from outside, then referral is beneficial.

In all, the assessment of when to involve outside help is a matter for a counsellor's judgement, rather than for a precise objective rule book. We can, however, distinguish two general categories of cases in each of which one factor can influence that judgement fairly decisively. These are:

 a. Cases which appear to contain a problem of personal adjustment.

 b. Cases which appear to contain a material need problem in the client's family.

In the first group, the decision to seek outside help would be settled if the client showed no signs of recovering from his state of stress or anxiety. To refer back to the young man in Chapter III, if he had not begun to show signs of returning to his normal pattern of behaviour after three or four sessions, I should have sought guidance about him for myself before doing anything else. In a phrase, counsellors must be governed by an awareness of their clients' states in the light of their experience, but not stampeded into hasty action by their own anxieties.

In the second group, a request for help or a positive response to a suggestion by the counsellor that it was available if needed would lead to a decision in favour of referral. The case at the end of Chapter IV, the boy who spent periods of alleged illness doing family jobs, illustrates this. He accepted with relief and enthusiasm the offer of help from other agencies, but this was not in any sense thrust upon him.

The 'when' of referral brings other issues in its train which underline the lack of precision about it. These concern both the counsellor's and the client's feelings when the counsellor refers his client to another agency, and the latter takes over. The counsellor, with whom his client has made a relationship of some value, is now likely to withdraw from the case. The client himself may feel rejected, despite the fact that he has accepted the idea of more specialized help and has asked for it himself. A useful general principle here is that the counsellor should 'leave well alone', and not interfere in the new agency's handling of the problem. He may indeed see his erstwhile client for a few moments in passing from time to time, simply to show his continuing interest and to let the client feel that he is not forgotten. This is no more than simple human concern, and it can be reassuring. He should not, however, continue to counsel unless the agency concerned asks his help at some stage in their operations. Given the reassurance that he has not been forgotten, a client finds it less confusing to deal with a representative of one agency than to cope with two or more people. Ultimately, he may well transfer his relationship from the counsellor to the new person. At this stage the counsellor is in a sense rejected himself, and the case is terminated as far as he is concerned. The most useful thing for him to do is to look back upon the case and survey his part in it critically, storing the experience and the analysis away for future reference in similar cases. He must not maintain his interest simply to satisfy his own curiosity or emotional needs or resent the fact that he is no longer needed.

These factors are especially important when dealing with

L

cases in which referral has been made to medical or psychological specialists. Here it may be disadvantageous or actually
dangerous for a counsellor to continue to see his client, when the
latter is undergoing specialist treatment. Specialists do not
want to have anxious counsellors to deal with as well as disturbed
clients. Here again, of course, if the specialist asks the counsellor
to keep in touch with the client he should do so, because the
specialist sees some benefit for the client in the contact being
maintained. Otherwise he must withdraw so that his client
shall not be confused by the activities of two different people
a confusion which will not help him at all. The emotional
anxieties of his counsellor may add substantially to a client's
confusion and offset any benefit accruing from specialist
treatment.

When a client is referred, and ultimately transferred to the
care and resources of another agency, for specialist treatment
or material provision, the counsellor's task is complete. He
withdraws and the case is terminated. Counsellors have here
to accept the fact that someone else knows better how to meet
the needs of the case than he does. Perhaps this is an experience
which teachers will not always find easily acceptable. For
example, many of them still resent it when a favoured pupil
elects to drop their subject in the curriculum. The determining
factor in the counselling or the teaching sense is simply what
is best for the client's future and total health as a whole person.
Nothing less than this is important. The teacher-counsellor's
ability to accept withdrawal and termination, not as rejection
of himself, but as a further expression of concern for his client,
can in fact add to the client's appreciation of his services. This
appreciation, however, is not a factor which should be considered at all by a counsellor when deciding whether to refer a
case or not.

Hitherto we have not mentioned the value of colleagues
within the school who can help a counsellor. This requires only
a brief reference, for every teacher-counsellor worth his salt
ought to be fully acquainted with the knowledge and experience

which his colleagues possess and know them well enough to call upon their services when the occasion is appropriate in the course of his counselling work.

Teacher-counsellors should not hesitate in helping their clients to make contacts with staff colleagues who can provide knowledge and express opinions which might be useful. Such colleagues obviously include those who take a special interest in careers guidance, and in further and higher education opportunities. Departmental heads and others who advise on subject choice and its relevance to career possibilities have also a contribution to make. No client, however, should be forced to consult his counsellor's colleagues. After all it is the client who has chosen to make a relationship with the counsellor and it is for him to decide when he feels secure enough to make one with someone else for whom his personal regard has hitherto been, for example, marked by fear rather than respect. The time commonly comes, however, when a client will ask for help beyond that which his counsellor can give. He may even realize that his counsellor can help him no more but be chary of asking if anyone else can do so. At this point a gentle suggestion from the counsellor may be all that is needed to make him go to someone else. Whether the counsellor acts as an intermediary is for him and the client to decide.

Similar considerations apply to involving teacher home-visitors, but even greater care needs to be exercised here. The real speciality of counsellors is making relationships of sincerity and reliability with clients; they are not snoopers upon or intruders into the privacy of other people's home life. Some young people resent the prospect of school staff visiting their homes, others welcome it. There is a similar diversity of view among parents. The reasons for the resentment are not always evident. Some clients may simply want to keep home and school separate. Others may be sensitive about deficiencies at home, real or imagined, and not wish to betray their homes by revealing the deficiencies at school. A client may also feel that a counsellor is his own personal friend and confidant, not to be shared with anyone at home: he may also be confused by the counsellor's contact with his parents and wonder 'whose side' the counsellor is on even if this is an over-simplification of a complex relationship pattern. It may emerge during counselling that something is seriously amiss at home, that even the parents may need some sort of treatment for which help may be secured at the relevant time, from appropriate agencies.

When young clients break down emotionally, as they sometimes do, it is not always easy to resist the temptation to send home visitors round, overruling the client's protestations. This temptation must, however, be resisted. Visits by teachers must not be thrust upon youngsters who express strong objections. Here we should remember that if home visiting or practical help is needed agencies outside schools can offer visits and other services more effectively and confidentially in a given case because the discreet people employed are not teachers, and because their findings are, therefore, much less likely to become public knowledge inside the school. So it is sometimes necessary to tell an anxious client that confidential help is available independently of the school. We shall look at this help in more detail in later pages.

Thus in all these facets of help from within a school's staff resources, clients' wishes and feelings must be respected in the privacy of counselling. Appointments with staff colleagues, and arrangements to visit homes should only be made with the client's agreement free from any pressure. Moreover the normal courtesy of giving plenty of notice of visits and appointments should be observed. In the end, however, a counsellor who has put a client in touch with colleagues is quite likely to find that his own relationship with the client will terminate, and he will have to withdraw, just as he has to do when some external agency is involved. This is simply an admission that he has done his job by helping his client towards maturity and responsibility and in improving relationships within the school. Considerations of his own importance do not matter. What is best for the client overrules any other consideration.

When to refer a client to someone else must seem to be surrounded by an aura of vague generalities. Let us therefore refer again to Mr Feather's remarks about management involving decisions upon whatever evidence is available in relation to the aims in view. We have to admit that while the aim of counselling is the general wellbeing of the client, definitive evidence which is available about how to achieve this is sparse indeed. Clearly defined rules are not available; indeed they are scarcely likely ever to be, counselling being the complex interpersonal relationship that it is. Thus all we have been able to provide is a general set of guide-lines to help a counsellor to use his own judgement about when to refer a client, guide lines modified by his understanding of each client in the particular circumstances which relate to him. Each new case presents him with knowledge and experience which simply add to his own personal 'guide book'. Counsellors however, cannot 'work according to the book', even if the book is their own. To adhere rigidly to any set of rules puts a client's interests second to the enforcement of rules and the application of procedures. Every case is different.

4 *How to refer*

It is a *sine qua non* that we cannot refer clients unless we know the people or organizations to which they can be referred. Counsellors should therefore familiarize themselves with the variety of social agencies and people to whom they are likely to refer clients in their schools' localities. We can, however, recognize two general classes of agency as a start; those who visit the school regularly under normal circumstances and those who do not.

a. AGENCIES WHICH VISIT A SCHOOL REGULARLY. Every school has supporting services represented by:

the school nurse
the school welfare officer
the youth employment officer.

Of these the first two can supply useful information about the home and family situation. They are often well-known figures to families who are in difficulty and visits from them are unlikely to cause the stress of resentment which a visit from a member of the teaching staff might create. They are professional in their own right, and often overloaded with cases especially in larger towns and cities. Their time should not be wasted by hasty referral for action in cases where the client needs support from his counsellors rather than actual help from one of them. Co-operation with them will save a great deal of unnecessary trouble. So often they have information which a counsellor might want to check or obtain. Whether the newly emerging figure of the teacher-social worker will solve problems which are not solved by these competent people has yet to be proved. Some teachers imbued with the social-worker urge feel that having home-visiting social workers on the staff means that visits can be paid immediately a crisis or problem turns up, rather than delay occurring because the welfare officer or nurse is too busy. The latter may have his or her own sense of priorities in the cases on his list, which may differ from that of the teachers in a particular school who naturally lay emphasis on their own pupils. We must, I think, reserve judgement on the wisdom of *always* having the same person both visiting the home and teaching a youngster who lives in it. We do not know yet how far an adolescent's sense of privacy is outraged by this arrangement. Parents certainly feel this at times.* All we can say at the moment is that a great deal of practical experience and evaluation – the latter itself a very difficult matter indeed – is needed before final decisions are made. At the moment, my impression is that youngsters seem to be happier when two different people do two different jobs. The counsel-

* *Educational Research News*, No. 9, May 1970; 'School and Home Liaison'.

lor's role as the client's private support and guide to personal responsibility is not confused in the latter's mind by home visiting by the counsellor

The youth employment officer is in a different category from the other two. His function is a very specialized one concerned with school leavers, and the preparation for leaving school. Moreover his normal point of contact should be the careers staff in a school. Counsellors should not take over the careers staff's role, but refer students who want guidance to them, with the appropriate introductory note or preliminary chat before the young man or woman turns up. As far as the youth employment service is concerned, therefore, counsellors are likely to be involved with them only at second hand unless their terms of reference specifically include career guidance in which they have been trained.

b. AGENCIES WHICH DO NOT VISIT SCHOOLS REGULARLY. Among these we can include the following:

i. School health and child guidance services which offer specialized help in health, behaviour problems, performance levels, and cognate matters.

ii. Children's departments and child and family welfare services, which can provide help to children and families in difficulty.

iii. Youth and community services which offer young people the opportunity of giving service to the community or neighbourhood in which they live.

iv. Probation and police liaison services (where the latter exist) which offer guidance services mainly to those who are stepping beyond the law.

v. Voluntary social services which offer a variety of skilled help.

As part of familiarizing themselves with the agencies available for support, counsellors in schools will find it most useful to make personal contact with someone in each of these services. This gives counsellors that feeling of security which comes from knowing someone who is an expert in a particular field of social service, and can advise them as well as providing specialist help directly to a client or his family if this is appropriate. Contacts are useful too in advising counsellors on the correct way of involving the organizations in a given case. It is also, I think, fair to say that they will appreciate two services which a counsellor can give to them. The first is that he can act as a filter through whom cases pass: often he may provide remedial support which a client needs himself, without directly involving the service. The second is that if the service has to be directly involved, a counsellor can provide lucid reports and documentation about a case, which makes the task of the service concerned a great deal easier. Nearly all these services are overloaded and some of the work which comes their way might well be dealt with quite effectively by a counsellor in school, especially when the latter knows that he can call on their advice and guidance if he feels that he is 'getting a little out of his depth'. A personal relationship between counsellor and someone in a given service is therefore extremely useful, especially when the agency realizes that the counsellor's judgement can be trusted.

Probation and the police liaison service deserve a special comment. Although it is no longer unusual for boys in school to be on probation, there are still schools in which students who are on probation are simply rejected. Apart from any other considerations, this makes a probationary period less effective than it ought to be, and the fault does not lie with the probation service. *One* person in a school, other than the head, ought to know when a student is on probation, and should work in collaboration with the probation officer in charge of a particular probationer. The latter then knows that his period of probation is to be taken seriously and that his work and attitude in school are both important to him and will be taken into account. It is equally important that this information should be confined generally to *one* person in the school, and not spread around so that others in the school may make defamatory remarks. No one is better fitted for this kind of work than a counsellor. Probation is an attempt at rehabilitation, should be treated as such, and its purpose recognized. Counsellors and probation officers can materially assist one another, quietly and confidentially, in making the most of the opportunities which this service offers to youngsters who might otherwise step further into a life of crime.

The police liaison service was introduced specifically for dealing with young first offenders using carefully selected police officers. The intention is not to bring such offenders before the courts – thus giving them an official criminal record, but to have them officially cautioned by a senior uniformed police officer. This rather unique service was first introduced in Liverpool some years ago, but it is not yet adopted by every police force. There is still some argument about its merits and effectiveness, but a comparable scheme was quite recently started by the Metropolitan Police Force. In this enterprise the police co-operate not only with parents and schools but with any agency which can help them to understand the background and influences affecting a particular juvenile. In so doing they help to dispel the common image of the police force as a harrier of young people: and this is a valuable by-product of a service, the aim of which is to prevent youngsters slipping into habitual crime. Counsellors may depend upon the co-operative advice and discretion of the police officers engaged in this service, whose character and dedication not only help young people but enhance good relations between public and police. Clearly, however, their particular services will only be required when clients seem to be on the verge of criminal activity.

The voluntary social services are in a category on their own, although they often co-operate with, and their help is sought by, the local statutory services already mentioned. Every community, large or small, has its voluntary services whose work is undertaken by dedicated and often highly skilled people, who display a professionalism far removed from the traditional image of the bountiful middle-class 'do-gooder'. They are expert in their field but their range of activities vary with the community. Counsellors who are not acquainted with the voluntary services available in their neighbourhood can ascertain which exists and what each does through the local Council of Social Service or the Citizens Advice Bureaux.

As in the case of the statutory agencies, they should make personal contact with someone in the voluntary services which offer a potentially useful service.

c. REFERRAL ACTION. Given the decision to seek support for himself, or direct help for a client, the sheer mechanics of referral are the easiest part of a counsellor's work. A telephone call or a brief note asking for an appointment to discuss a case is all that is required. This gives the agency the gist of the case, and enables it in consultation with the counsellor to decide whether to take the case over or leave it with him, while providing him with guidance and support. I have already stated that some agencies listed are overloaded. They will be happier to assist a counsellor with some of his cases rather than take over, so that they can devote their specialist attention to the really serious cases which come to their attention. If counsellor and agency agree that the latter should take over, the counsellor will need to prepare a lucid, concise and relevant report on which the agency can act. If an agency takes over, the case is terminated as far as the counsellor is concerned, unless he is specifically asked by the agency to continue to co-operate. If counselling in schools expands and collaboration with agencies consequently develops, we might expect such co-operation to continue in certain cases while the agency is taking action, so that the counsellor can support his client and help him to understand what his happening, as long as he needs that support and help.

d. CO-OPERATION WITH PARENTS. If a counsellor consults another agency purely for his own guidance, it is quite unnecessary for him to involve the client's parents, and we need say no more in this case. The situation is quite different, however, if the considered opinion of a counsellor and agency working together is that the latter should take over. The client's parents must now be involved, certainly to the point of being invited to co-operate – as most of them do. We can differentiate here between two general types of client. The first of these are those whose health, behaviour and achievement as seen by the school seem to justify formal consultation with a view to treatment. The second are those whose material deprivation or domestic mismanagement, for whatever reason, is such as to justify practical aid to the home.

In the first category the best approach is to invite the parents to come to school and discuss their child's difficulties. If it is not otherwise possible this must be arranged out of school hours. In the course of the discussion it falls to the counsellor to convince the parents that specialist advice and treatment is in the best interests of both their child and themselves. The head of the school, or his assigned representative such as the head of the boys' house, wing or other school division should be present, having seen the confidential report on which the recommendations are based and agreed to the action intended. From this point onwards it is for the agency concerned to arrange specialist appointments and to refer back to the school if necessary. Home visiting agencies can then be involved to assist parents in making the necessary arrangements.

In the second category the school welfare service or the school nurse may be invited to help. Alternatively if a school staff includes one or two teacher-social workers who are allowed time for home visiting, they may be involved if family and client agree. All these people can make a relationship with the parents and family by visiting, and arrange whatever practical help is necessary. The counsellor's function is less immediately practical: it is to satisfy the psychological needs of the client for a relationship with someone outside the family. Home-visitor and counsellor thus work in partnership satisfying the different needs of two different sorts of people.

Some attention has been devoted in these pages to various aspects of referral and the co-operation with other agencies which it entails. It should not be inferred from this that referral will often be necessary. Neither the problems which make it necessary nor the procedural detail it requires will conform to a standard pattern. The chart on p. 147, however, presents a suggested scheme of communication for counsellors who have referral problems.

Preconceived notions about a client's needs in referral are to be avoided at all costs. A counsellor may be presented with a client's statement which at first suggests referral to one agency, but further enquiry may reveal that a different one is much more appropriate. Petty theft is not always a matter for the law: welfare services may be more helpful. What appears to be at first behavioural disturbance is not always a subject for referral to psychological guidance agencies: counselling or curricular or careers advice in the school may be more beneficial. We simply do not know until we have got to know our clients. The situations presented by clients in Birmingham may differ in general tenor from those in Brighton, those in Glasgow from those in Gloucester, those in Stepney from those in Stanmore, those in a new town from those in an old one, and those on a new housing estate from those in a down-town area. They will be influenced too by the atmosphere in a given school, for example, by whether staff-student relationships are formal or relaxed, or whether a school council exists and works well. All manner of family, environmental and neighbourhood influences affect the range and type of work which may come the way of a teacher-counsellor, and the agencies with which he has most often to co-operate in referral. His clients will not, however, expect him to satisfy their needs by administrative efficiency in speedy referral after a rather superficial and inadequate five-minute interview. The common denominator of every counsellor's work is his attitude to the people who come to him, and the relationships he makes with them. More often than not agencies to which he can refer will buttress and guide him,

and give him confidence to do his own job in the security which
their existence and skill provide for him. Very speedy referral
may be regarded by clients as a hint that the counsellor really
has no time for them, and is not up to his job. Procedural
skill in referral is, in all, not a substitute for concern, patience
and sensitive judgement.

The successful use of referral depends first upon rational
decision within a school about the management of counselling
and who is responsible for referring cases. It is conditional
thereafter upon the quality and competence of counsellors;
upon their knowledge and relationships with agencies which
can help in their work; upon their understanding the differences
between guidance for them and direct help to their clients;
upon their ability to withdraw from a case when an agency
takes over; upon their prudence and balanced judgement
rather than rigid adherence to administrative procedures; upon
their understanding of clients' needs in relation to the school
and neighbourhood; upon their appreciation of people's privacy
and the need to keep their referrals confidential. Given these
prerequisites, referral is a necessary adjunct of that growing
teamwork between schools and social agencies which can make
the future life of today's school population healthier in every
way, and teacher-counsellors should become recognized
participants in the case-conference technique which already
characterizes much social work outside school walls. Referral
is not, for all this, a means by which a counsellor avoids his
own responsibilities, or a way of unloading even more cases
on to agencies which are all too often heavily overloaded.

VI

Summary and prognostication

The concept of the teacher-counsellor is not yet a generally accepted feature of the educational landscape. Feelings about counselling seem to suggest indifference rather than specific attitudes for or against, if a recent study in *Educational Research** is a fair indication. Of the teachers who were invited to co-operate in this enquiry, eighty per cent did not bother to reply, but of those who did, a quarter felt that counselling would be better done by non-specialist teacher-counsellors than by specialists. A conference organized by *Forum* in June 1970 revealed some opposition to specialist snoopers impinging on teachers' concern for the problems of their pupils†, as well as some recognition of the value of really human counsellors. Whether the counselling plant is developing roots or not is difficult to assess, but if it is, teachers certainly need more explanation and enlightenment than are currently available to them in this country. In particular they want to know better what it is about, what it may or may not achieve, and some understanding of the problems which they, rightly or wrongly, anticipate will transpire if they turn to counselling as part of their job, or will arise if a counselling service is introduced into their schools. In this book I have attempted to deal with some of these problems.

In the preceding chapters I surveyed quite briefly the

* *'Teachers' attitudes to counselling and guidance'*, Lyon *et al. Educational Research*, June 1970.
† *New Society*, June 18th, 1970.

general concepts of counselling and its relation with a variety of cognate activities. Next I considered in some detail the so-called dual and triple roles, and the relation between these and the nature and structure of school authority both as the latter is and as many people imagine it to be. I am aware that my treatment disregarded the enlightenment about school authority which is slowly spreading through our educational system, but there is still abundant evidence in the press and elsewhere of formal rigidity in school authority which makes for difficulties when counselling is considered. The relationship between authority and the multiple roles is important, because integrated and experienced teachers who are likely to make good counsellors, are, in the nature of things, responsible for maintaining authority in schools. Problems of professional loyalty, personal anxiety within those who practice the dual and triple roles, as well as the problems of counselling management all arise here. I suggested, however, that duality is a phenomenon not confined to the special province of teacher-counsellors; that it runs through the whole fabric of living, in industry and parenthood, in science and religion, in the clash between historical habit and future progress. Adherents of any Christian persuasion may recall the Pauline duality and its searching conflict between the high and the lower life, while Marxists will not be unaware of the dualities which lie in their particular dialectic. There is a duality too, in the law, for the courts have a duty expressly put upon them not only to consider the retribution by which society expresses its disapproval of an offender's conduct, but also to understand the offender as a person and to see what can be done to rehabilitate him. And in domestic courts the element of sympathy and acceptance, of guidance and understanding must be high in the minds of those who have to administer within the framework of the law the tragic problems which often come to their attention. Legality is often a poor substitute for kindly personal relationships, and authority itself is not always effective in helping people to come to an understanding of their own difficulties and how to solve them.

By putting the special duality of the teacher-counsellor into a setting of a much more widespread duality, it was my contention that it will thus become less strange and more tolerable. It becomes no longer a unique phenomenon in itself but a special manifestation in a particular setting – the school – of something which pervades the whole of life and society and with which everyone has to live consciously or unconsciously. None the less, I expressed the view that senior and experienced teachers are bound to be sensitive to possible stresses and anxieties which practising the dual or triple roles in the traditionally authoritarian setting of a school seems likely to create. However, recognizing the reality or the possibility of these stresses and anxieties is the first step towards that personal adjustment which makes them tolerable and to the management decisions which make sustaining the two roles feasible. In other words the viability of the two roles is closely related to the personality characteristics of the practitioners and the climate in which they work. It is worth noting here that living with stress and anxiety is not something which is confined to teacher-counsellors: it is one of the concomitants of living in our modern sophisticated society. I also suggested that doubts about the viability seem to lie more in teachers' minds, than they do in the minds of their potential clients, some of whom at least seem to be able to understand and tolerate them.

When I looked at school authority, I made a distinction between the general conceptions of law and order in society and the special provisions which schools make in order to discharge the duties which society puts upon them, and achieve their goals. In passing, there is now some notable confusion about what these duties or goals really are. The special provisions, therefore are very much open to challenge and I raised a number of questions about the structure of school authority and the regulations made to support and enforce it. These have been raised by other people on a number of occasions; but the answers, like those to the problems of the dual role, lie within the minds of teachers who want to embark on counselling. They cannot be imposed upon individual teachers. At various stages it may have seemed as if I condemned out of hand every one of the practices I scrutinized. We should remind ourselves, however, that the comprehensive question at issue is not abolishing or retaining rules and regulations, but whether these are habitual and historical or rational and relevant in relation to the social context in which education is conducted today. A salient feature of that context is that the top ends of our secondary schools contain not children but young adults many of whom will be legally adult before they leave. We have to accept that fact. These young adults now have a stronger entitlement to question rules; equally I would counsel them that they also have a duty to accept more responsibility. They ask, as I have in effect asked, first, why we do what we do about authority in school, secondly, whether the reasons for doing so are good ones, and thirdly, whether there are not better reasons for doing things differently.

Because counsellors ask this kind of question of themselves and their clients, seeking greater rationality in the structure of authority, and encouraging greater self-control and responsibility in their clients, they actually strengthen authority. Moreover, their own authority stems from them being the sort people they are and conducting themselves in the way they do. It is not positional: it is personal, and independent of their position in the school hierarchy. Moreover it seems to be greater because it is attributed to them by their clients through the medium of the relationships they make with the latter. Their authority is not an imposed one and is thus less easily assailed. If this is so then their influence tends to extend outside the counselling room throughout the whole operational matrix of the school, a view supported by a recent account of counselling experience.* Even so, teacher-counsellors – especially those playing the triple role – must be tuned to accepting what, for want of a better term, I called 'failure' in the special sense

* Andrew Finch, Head of Longslade Upper School, Leicestershire: *Forum*, June 1970.

M

of dealing with clients who seemed not to respond, at a particular point in time and personal growth to their counsellor's particular brand of personal therapy. Here again, teachers in the traditional sense have to tolerate this, in the limited field of academic work. The deeper involvement of the counselling relationship can only enhance this tolerance and improve our understanding of work-failure. This, however, must not blind counsellors to the need for constant examination of their approach and method in the light of their so-called failures.

Lastly I turned to referral. Here knowledge of possible sources of support is a buttress on its own to a counsellor, not because he will always need to use them, but because he gains confidence from the fact there are other people to whom he can turn either for his own guidance, or direct action with a client if he needs to. The greatest benefits from referral are realized when counsellors have good personal relationships with people in the agencies which they feel they are likely to involve. If there is a danger in referral it lies in excessive use of it. Transferring a client to someone else whom he does not know personally may do him more harm than good unless it is based on need and careful preparation. Finally referral can exact a sacrifice from a counsellor in that it may require him to withdraw from a given case entirely. On the other hand, when referral is made to a welfare officer or a home-visiting teacher it may be helpful for the counsellor to continue to support his client while the social worker colleague supports the client's family. Whatever the final decision about handling a given case may be, referral is not a substitute for a counsellors' personal attributes or the relationships he makes with his clients. The great majority of them will come to him because he is the sort of person he seems to them to be, not because they expect to be passed on to someone else in a blaze of administrative efficiency. Those who think that they need expert advice from some person outside the school when they first approach a counsellor are more likely than not to find that they can cope with their situations themselves because his reception accords to them a confidence and a competence which they had not thought they possessed up to the point of meeting him. In other words, referral is not a substitute for the quality of counsellors and their attitude to clients.

All this comprises a summary of the topics with which I have dealt in preceding pages. I have not taken into account the broader educational or philosophical significance of counselling at all. At this stage therefore, and by way of conclusion, let us refocus our thoughts on the real priority of counselling, and consider briefly how this relates if at all to educational thought in general, seeking perhaps further justification for it.

In the introduction I wrote that this book is based upon my own personal experience, and conversations with other teachers. The latter's attitudes to counselling varied from the enthusiastic to the sceptical. In passing, some of the sceptics might well make better counsellors than the enthusiasts; for the latter's warm but emotional reaction to the prospect of closer relationships with their students seemed often to sweep the need for constant self-appraisal out of their minds. Whatever our views may be about the structural detail of authority, the complexities of the dual and triple roles, or the relationships and administrative mechanisms of referral, the constant theme of all this discussion has been that counselling is indispensably about people, their situations, attitudes and feelings and relationships. It is not primarily concerned with maintaining a well-lubricated machine of social administration, or providing agreeable academic debate about abstract concepts, or maintaining the fabric of school authority. This is not to say that it does not require good management or clear thinking. On the contrary my intention has been to make clear that it does; without these it cannot provide a service which meets the needs of clients. We must have sensible but minimal management and rigorous self-critical thinking about the things which counsellors are essaying, what their attitudes are, and why. My purpose is not to denigrate management and analysis, but to establish beyond doubt the priority of counselling. For two characteristics mark, indeed almost bedevil, much contemporary debate about counselling, and obscure this priority. The first of these is a tendency to over-intellectualize counselling, and the second a proclivity rigidly to over-organize it: the real priority is to humanize it.

By over-intellectualizing I mean that we may, if we are not very careful, treat counselling as a concept, an idea about which we may hold interesting and pleasant discussion on matters of theory far removed from the realities of the client in trouble. Rigorous intellectual discipline is certainly a necessary counterblast to the very real dangers inherent in the emotional enthusiasm which seems to overcome some teachers when counselling is mentioned. There are, however, equal dangers in treating people and their problems merely as ideas: as a result we forget that we counsel individual human beings who are in varying degrees of personal distraction. Moreover over-indulgence in conceptualization can bring in train a blunting of the acute perception and sensitivity which a counsellor offers to his clients in meeting their several needs. Furthermore, adherence to existing concepts reduces our receptiveness to new ones, especially in the behavioural sciences, or the generalities which lie behind the concepts. To digress for a moment, the history of physical science is full of the obstruction to progress which followed an over-zealous devotion to rigid concepts which existed at the material time. The assortment of particles of which matter is constructed – electrons, protons and the rest – are concepts. These are useful to explain certain observed phenomena. Yet at various points in the time for which their existence has been recognized, it has seemed as though they have obeyed certain rigid rules. It was often felt that observations had to comply with the rules; and if these really did not meet a particular case, much time and argument had to be devoted to modifying the rules. Few laws are fundamentally peculiar to them: rather do they comply with the more generalized laws of thermodynamics and disorder which operate on the particles in any given environment. The special characteristics of the latter may modify the workings of the general laws. If this underlying generality is applied to the concept of the relationship between client and counsellor we can understand that this relationship is far from constant in all respects for every counsellor and every client. We may indeed say with confidence that privacy between counsellor and client, and acceptance of the latter by the former are governing principles of every individual relationship, just as mass and electric charge are dominating parameters of every electron in any situation.

We must however admit that these features of counselling are overshadowed by the influence of specific factors appertaining to a given relationship; these include the client's social situation and feelings, the precise moment in his life at which he avails himself of counselling, the individual personalities of client and counsellor. These determine and modify in individual counselling relationships the way in which counselling proceeds in detail, the time it takes, and what action, if any, is taken by a counsellor in consulting other people or organizations. They are but three of the particular factors which affect counselling, just as the immediate environment conditions of time, energy and other physical factors ultimately determine the specific behaviour of physical particles. Highly detailed theoretical concepts which the history of other fields of human activity suggests lack real permanence, have to be replaced in counselling by specific information about a particular case. There are no detailed prescriptions for an infinitely variable range of situations. Neither are there any substitutes for the counsellor's own human sensitivity and understanding. These enable him to meet the challenge of change imperturbably. They are the constants he brings to a limitless variety of clients.

By over-organizing counselling, I mean that we pay undue attention to rigid management and organizational structures. We are agreed that decisions have to be made about who counsels, who organizes referrals and arranges channels of communication within a school. It is rigid conformity with the unalterable minutiae of administration which blocks the human operation of a counselling service; and because retreat into problems of organization is a useful device for impeding change I sometimes think that insistence on administrative details by teachers indicates that they have strong feelings of conservatism and insecurity about counselling. When they ask, as they have asked, how many clients per week can be expected, how counselling is related to house or year systems, the average length of interview, how much time should be allocated to counselling and on which days, they are really asking the wrong questions and evading the right ones. If teachers are looking at counselling for the first time, the really important questions should be put to themselves and be something like these:

1. Why do we want to counsel?

2. Why do we think we are the right kind of people to counsel?

3. Are we in fact the right sort of people to counsel?

These are difficult questions to answer. The responses lie within the character and personalities of the questioners, and are to be dealt with by selection procedures.

At this point a brief comment on selection may be useful. Since *Teachers as Counsellors* was written there has been a perceptible movement towards self-selection processes. In these teachers decide to train for counselling, education in personal relationships and related activities, but have the facility of opting-out if they find that the situations presented to them during that training are not acceptable to them. I have certainly found teachers, and others engaged in work with young people, who admit that counselling had turned out during training to be something with which they could not cope. They deserve high praise for recognizing their unsuitability. There are, however, still those who persist despite the stress to which the work subjects them and some kind of superintendence of their work still seems desirable especially if formal selection methods are abandoned. It is fair to state, however, that here we are still feeling our way carefully. Experience will be helpful, but on balance I feel that a selection procedure and careful observation during training are necessary in addition to any self-selection by individual teachers.

To emphasize the importance of proper balance between client needs on one hand and intellectual or procedural needs on the other let me return briefly to the young man who walked out of an examination room in a state of mental stress: he was in no mood for form-filling or being told it was an inconvenient time to come, or the wrong way to go about seeking an interview. Neither did he want intellectual discussion about what was the matter with him. He wanted someone to talk to at that moment in time: nothing more or less. He may owe the early return of his customary sang-froid to the member of the school secretarial staff who found him dazed and waiting outside my office and searched for me round the school, for the simple reason that I could and would accept him as he was at that moment. Anyone else who was capable of doing this would have performed the same useful service for him. Counselling provided a response to his needs when it was called upon to do so. Intellectual concepts and management structure were irrelevant to his needs.

This particular case, of course, raises the problem of time. What would I have done had I been teaching when the young man's plight was notified to me? What would I have done with the class? The answer is simple enough. It is to do what any senior experienced teacher has to do when he is called urgently away, as he often is, to the telephone or some other pressing school business. I should have set the class some work to do, told the man in the next room that I had been called away urgently and seen the client. Having seen him I could then have assessed whether he needed a long chat immediately, or whether he could wait, after I had seen him for five or ten minutes. Coping with disturbance to teaching seems to me to be part of a teacher's life anyway, and counsellor-training can only help him to live with it. Some people may throw up their arms in horror at the thought that a class can be left. Of course there are classes which cannot be left, but these are fewer than we imagine, provided that the relationship between them and the teacher is right. Yet if a given class is so irresponsible with him as to need constant supervision by a particular teacher it is difficult to escape the conclusion that such a teacher is most unlikely to be suitable for counselling. Moreover, if relationships among the staff are so bad that it is impossible to obtain help from a colleague in any situation resembling the one specifically described, then it seems extremely unlikely that a counselling service could exist within the school concerned. Certainly, teachers who counsel ought to have some extra free time, so that they can make appointments to see clients, but the whole timetable should not be disrupted or complicated simply to meet their convenience, and how much time is for those who manage a given school to decide in the light of their own and other's experience. Perhaps one period a day would be a useful starting allocation.

Counselling at the level with which I am concerned in this book and in *Teachers as Counsellors* is best described as a pragmatic experience disciplined by the counsellor's own sensitivity and awareness of his own frailty. Much of it is very uncomplicated conversation in private on terms of equality. The counsellor's ability to care and his personal sensitivity and perception must not be sullied by self-satisfying emotional urges which make counselling more important to his well-being than it is to the client's. This potentially self-indulgent and possibly dangerous aspect of a teacher-counsellor's activity is one to which some specialist practitioners in the behavioural sciences would certainly draw attention; and in support of it, they would demand a searching selection procedure in the light of their experience of teachers whose unsuitability for counselling was clear – except to themselves. Here another counselling priority

emerges: namely, that concepts of counselling and its management are secondary to the quality of counsellors. Quality in
this context means, *inter alia*, an ability to deal with totally
unforeseen and unexpected situations without deeply preconceived notions or any sign of external alarm. It is in the sense
of dealing with such situations that I call counselling a pragmatic experience.

The word 'pragmatic' brings into focus the whole philosophy
of counselling in a part of the total educative process. We can
of course lose sight of the essentially person-to-person relationship of counselling in a miasma of philosophical discussion as
easily as in the other ways I have mentioned. Yet counselling
and its related services bid fair to become acceptable parts
of the whole learning and educational process. It is instructive
to see, therefore, how much of the philosophy of counselling
is already part of the history of educational philosophy. The
teacher's task 'however little he may know it, is to direct the
pupil to foregather with himself, and, in the chambers of his
mind, find the truth which is there'.* Thus wrote St Augustine,
who saw the teacher's job as stimulating pupils to learn, as a
counsellor does with his clients, although in the latter's sphere of
operations the learning is about the client's self. St Thomas
Aquinas used the analogy of the doctor who really assists his
patient to cure himself; teachers must stimulate their pupils
to learn and gain a knowledge of truth. They must also realize
that human beings such as their pupils are not just baskets to
be filled with knowledge. This direction to the significance
of pupils as individuals was repeated in much later years
especially by Rousseau, Pestalozzi, Herbart, Froebel and
Piaget. Sir John Adams' bipolar theory of learning in which he
used the terms 'educator' and 'educand' instead of teacher and
pupil, underlay his thesis that education is a much wider
conception than teaching and that the educator or teacher is

---

* Quoted in *A Monument to St Augustine* by Father M. D. D'Arcy, in an
essay, 'The Philosophy of St Augustine', Sheed and Ward, 1934, p. 178.

N

the means by which the educand or pupil educates himself. The modern schools of existentialist or personalist philosophy influence educational thought in the same way because they emphasize the value of individual human beings. The founder, Søren Kierkegaard, expressed his views a hundred years ago when the industrial revolution was accompanied by an obvious propensity for degrading human beings as a result of subjugating them to the squalid demands of an industrialized society. That they have come to the fore in the last twenty-five years is probably due to the appalling ravages of war in the twentieth century, and the accelerating tendency in that period to make individuals vassals of political or industrial systems. Such a depersonalization of individuals applies equally to an educational system in which students see themselves as pawns in an examination game or forced conformists to irrational structures of school authority. Perhaps the most fascinating and significant feature of these philosophies is that their exponents include thinkers from every European religious persuasion, from Roman Catholic (Roman Marcel), Jewish (Martin Buber) and Russian Orthodox (Nicholas Berdyaev) to agnostic and atheist (Martin Heidegger and Jean-Paul Sartre) as well as Kierkegaard himself who was a Danish Lutheran. It is beside the point in this book to argue whether these people are justifiably grouped together as existentialists or whether some are 'existentialists' and others 'personalists'. The material point is that they all represent a revolt against one facet or another of the objective and determinist view of human life and society favoured by Descartes and well expressed by Laplace* 'An intelligence . . . would be able to comprehend the motions of the largest bodies of the world and those of the lightest atoms in one single formula, provided his intellect were powerful enough to subject all data to analysis: to him nothing would be uncertain. Both past and future would be present in his eye.' This, in the scientific euphoria of the nineteenth century,

* *The Origin and Growth of Physical Science*: vol II. Hurd and Hatfield, Pelican, p. 319.

applied to human beings as much as it did to inanimate matter. Perhaps the clearest expression of the opposite view is that of the Jewish thinker Martin Buber, in his remarkable work *Between Man and Man.** This extends the anti-determinist thinking of the personalist and existentialist philosophers who had gone before him. For him the central feature of the educational process is the 'I-thou' – rather than the 'I-it' – relationship between teacher and pupil. This relationship has to be such that there is a continuing dialogue between teacher and pupil in which the latter's influence must be not too obvious and must enable the relationship between the two people to evolve into a friendship without which the pupil cannot be properly educated. Education for Buber is dependent upon a meeting of two persons. The resemblance to the client-counsellor relationship is very marked. Finally the word 'pragmatic' conjures up the opinions of J. Dewey† one of whose comments is particularly relevant in the present context. A teacher 'must, in addition, have a sympathetic understanding of individuals as individuals which gives him an idea of what is actually going on in the minds of those who are learning'. Teachers, Dewey felt, needed to be counsellors and friends, as well as instructors and stage managers.

I realize that this brief selection of opinion from the history of educational philosophy is such as to invite a charge of special pleading. None the less it must suggest that the sensitivity of the counsellor's approach to his job has a well documented and respectable pedigree. Moreover it must make us all pause and ponder seriously whether counselling, in the sense of making a sensitive personal relation between teacher and taught based upon mutual respect and understanding, is as new in principle as some people would have us believe. Neither in the light of this evidence, are the advocates of counselling far removed from the age-long mainstreams of educational thought. Clearly a great weight of scholarly authority lies

---

* No. 12 in Suggestions for further reading.
† *Experience and Education*, Macmillan: New York, p. 33.

behind the counsellor's contention that it is individuals who matter, and their relationships which are influential. Moreover the modern movement towards educating the student's whole person which I mentioned in the introduction seems not in fact to be modern at all. It has been a central theme of educational thought for a very long time and enjoys the patronage of sages from a wide range of philosophical persuasions. The evolution of educational relationships towards complete partnership between teacher and pupil is thus something which has for long been advocated.

I am also aware that the consensus agreement about the value of people between these eminent authorities who are spread along the line of educational history is probably restricted to this very matter. Such agreement, for example, might not be found between the views of Dewey and St Thomas on external or ultimate values, for Dewey seems to have held the belief that values are what young people create for themselves by experiment. However, the general recognition by the authorities quoted of the importance of individual consciousness, dignity and value helps to create the framework of a sort of counsellor's faith. For this reason alone, the consensus is important. It does not really matter here that from Plato and Aristotle onwards, philosophers have rarely been able to agree about the broad aims of education; or that St Thomas Aquinas and Rousseau, if they had been able to meet, would have approached the subject from diametrically opposed standpoints. For broad agreement upon the value of people has a second advantage in that it gives a well-based historical platform from which we can move into new patterns of future educational relationships with some confidence because of the weight of opinion inherited from the past. Moreover, it gives teacher-counsellors what every teacher ought to have, namely a philosophy of his job. A man who has a philosophy is not easily distracted from his work, nor corrupted in his aims. It gives him the strength to survive criticism, to endure incompetence, to bear with appalling working conditions, and to tolerate the anxiety which accompanies very limited achievement of his goals.

It is difficult to define a counsellor's goals in the educational sense, but something like this is near to such a definition. By ascribing to his clients the dignity and worth which accrue from their existence and will he aims to help them to find within themselves the sources to deal with their problems and the capacity to accept themselves and their roles in life, and so to achieve that mental and sound health to which I have referred before. I referred also to educational goals in the discussion on authority in schools. Whether the dreary and often pointless habits of such authority achieve anything at all, let alone educational goals, is for readers to decide. It seems almost indisputable to me that the counsellor's approach is far more rewarding to the clients, if only because it brings them face to face with themselves in the security of a relationship which has nothing to do with dress or social class or school attainment. Our contemporary world is dominated, or so it seems to many young people, by an appalling technological and administrative depersonalization of human individuality, far worse than anything Kierkegaard imagined. Much student revolt is concerned with this, and drugs are an escape for some. Perhaps the counselling teacher can give his young clients the confidence in themselves to withstand the pressures of their environment because he seems to be secure himself, but not rigid or dogmatic. He is a point of stability and a supporter of individuality in an unstable and collectivized society. He can lead his clients in a school situation to understand that there is not really a conflict between freedom and authority; that there is rather a balance to be struck between freedom and authority; and that without some of the latter there can be none of the former, at least in our present stage of human imperfections. The teacher-counsellor can enhance his client's own wills to withstand the pressures which afflict them, because he seems to have the confidence to do so himself. Thus he is well placed to fight the battle for human individuality and worth which, whether teachers like it or not, has to be fought in schools as much as anywhere else, if it is to be fought at all.

But, some will say – and I have heard their voices often enough – all this philosophy and idealism is meaningless when teachers are confronted with rampant truancy, abundant thieving and violence on the doorstep: there is no time for self-sacrificing enquiry into why this kind of misconduct goes on, certainly not the amount of time which counsellors require. Indeed this is true, and I have already made two things plain. The first is that suppressing unlawful activity is a matter for the law-enforcing agencies, if it has spread beyond the control of school authority. The second is that no one can counsel adequately amidst chaos. Moreover, no advocate of counselling to my knowledge has said that it is an instant cure for anything: but it may help to recognize the psychopath, or the constantly anti-social youth and help them to the appropriate specialist agency. In addition one accruing benefit of counsellor training is that it enhances the capacity to remain unruffled and preserve morale in the face of highly stressed situations; and, as every teacher knows well, when the restless students realize they cannot upset him or 'get him on the run' as the vernacular has it, the battle for control is more than half won. The real danger, however, lies in this: that so often when some sort of so-called order has been restored after a temporary breakdown in control, the school authority fails to find out why the breakdown occurred in the first place. At this point the counsellor's work becomes invaluable, not as a law enforcer, but as a genuine enquirer into why what happened did happen. If one youth who is on probation responds to the joint treatment of his superintending officer and his teacher-counsellor working in harness in the long established appreciation of the worth of individuals which I have tried to illustrate in earlier pages, then the effort will have been worth while in both cash and human terms. Case conferences in schools under counsellor leadership could do more than is being done at present to detect and lead to the correction of pupils who are likely to err. The early signs of failing effort and deteriorating conduct are often there for us all to notice, if our minds are sharpened to do so. To look hard and long through a counsellor's eyes at the structure of school authority and organization might reveal in a given establishment that too much concern and effort is directed to the wrong things, which require so much energy in application and enforcement that we forget the purpose behind the establishment's existence. The latter is simply to develop a sense of personal responsibility in young people against all the odds, through the example of those who do not need to impose authority because it is attributed to them.

Perhaps I pay too much attention to the lawless, the inadequate and the anti-social. For them the welfare officer and the home-visitor are perhaps more appropriate. Counselling is concerned with them no more than any other section of the community. It is simply about people – any people. It is applicable to all because it can fulfil the psychological and personal needs of anyone, regardless of ability or background: the slow developer and the brilliant linguist, students from affluent suburbia, a new housing estate, or a down-town slum – for all of these may share a deprivation not expressible in material terms, but displaying itself as a loss of personal identity, a sense of not belonging, a distaste for the world as they find it, or an inability to cope with the prospect before them and the choices they have to make. To correct these forms of deprivation, and any others that occur, is certainly one of a counsellor's educational goals: and if this goal is achieved, the other goals of work and job success and fulfilment are more likely to follow. Seen against this prospect of fuller personal development the matters with which we have been concerned in this book, authority, dual and triple role stresses and the mechanics of referral may seem almost trivial by comparison. None the less, if some people believe they matter, we must deal with them. And if we compare the counsellor's role, method and quality with the demands made upon teachers

who are, for example, involved in the Humanities Curriculum
Project, we may be surprised at the resemblance between them.
Lawrence Stenhouse, director of the project* wrote: 'We need
to create a new climate of relationships with adolescents
which takes account of their responsibility and is not authoritarian. Education must be founded on co-operation not coer-
cion. We must find a way of expressing our common humanity
with our pupils and we must be sensitive to the need to justify
the decisions of authority to those affected by them. . . . In
short we need to transform our adolescent pupils into students.'
I would extend this further and add 'and our students into
young adults'. He writes further: 'The teacher, although he be
neutral on controversial issues, has, as an educator, a responsibility to foster rationality rather than irrationality, sensitivity
rather than insensitivity, imaginativeness rather than unimag-
inativeness, tolerance rather than intolerance. He must also
help students to see that standards of critical judgement are
important.' All this is part of a counsellor's approach, and
suggests the extent to which new teaching methods and the
teacher qualities they demand resemble that approach and the
personal qualities which must accompany it and without which
the methods will fail. This is not all of counselling of course;
the latter goes deeper, and may involve the counseller pro-
foundly in reorientating a single human being to learn about
himself rather than about something. But the penetration of
teaching method by the sensitivity which marks the counsellor
is here continuing the thinking of the past in a way for all to
see who wish to. Yet the response by pupils or students will not
be quick: it will be guarded and cautious as people often are
to new explorations.

A fifth-former showing uncanny insight very recently drew
a rather startling but valid comparison between making
relaxed relationships between teacher and taught and a
remarkable programme on Independent Television which
presented the record of an expedition seeking to make contact

* 'Pupils into Students', *Schools Council News Letter* No. 5, pp. 10–11.

for the first time in history with a tribe, the Kreen Acrore in
the Amazonian jungle noted for their execution of intruders.
Three of these elusive people were seen at a distance but no
further contact ensued. The expedition left gifts for them
at a place away from the explorer's camp: these were taken,
and gifts in return were left for the expedition. The explorers
watched, waited and listened in the gloom and discomfort of
the rain forest for a tentative and dangerous contact with a
tribe whose isolation, perhaps for ten thousand years, had
made them suspicious of everyone. The explorers did not
impose themselves or search aggressively: their peaceful intentions and good faith had to be established beyond doubt in
the minds of those they sought to meet, despite acute discomfort, a sense of failure, and a sometimes failing morale. So
it is, on a different plane, with counselling. Students and
teachers are conditioned by one hundred years of universal
compulsory school authority in this country to be wary of
the open-ended relationships which counsellors offer. Counsellors can only watch and listen and wait, with wary calm
and patient interest, approaching with care, so that their
intentions too are established in good faith. The important
word perhaps is *faith* – in human beings. For this makes
disappointment and anxiety tolerable; it ensures that whatever
appreciation or success supervenes is a matter for nothing
more than humility; it keeps morale high. It helps us to
venture boldly like explorers into new territory and attempt
new relationships as a means of educating the young, not
only intellectually and vocationally, but also by leading them
towards that social and mental health which makes for a
fuller and less strained life and which is the entitlement of all.
Equally, just as venturing into the jungle requires as much
foresight, planning and prudent preparation for the unknown
as is possible, so too does counselling require thorough preparation on the part of those who venture into it; and once
counsellors are committed to an expedition into relationships
with their clients they must be willing and able to accept

whatever happens. They are not aiming at conformity in their clients, or taking the fire out of the latter's idealism. Their therapy is primarily that which comes from a dependable relationship. Even this, however, needs at times an explorer's nerve, and this is something teachers cannot afford to lose when they are challenged every day to seize opportunities for enhancing the dignity and value of people. Perhaps too, they need an explorer's courage to keep their educational sights on the goal of developing the self-respect and sense of responsibility of growing young men and women, instead of just filling their minds and telling them what to do, often without any obvious rational basis for doing so. They ought also to remember that they should not reject or cast out an individual as a person, because they have rejected something which that individual has done. None of us can survive that sort of judgement.

Counselling in British schools is still in the developmental stage: its evolution will follow different paths in different schools and social environments. Here and elsewhere it will be affected by national and racial cultures and traditions. Its therapy will not, however, depend upon its practitioners' several opinions about the various facets of school authority. Their capacity to tolerate criticism of them is significant; helping their clients to look at the realities of their own lives is vital. Whether those realities include enduring a harsh home, a conflict of racial, religious and cultural loyalties, the relative triviality of school tradition, or the stress of an examination system, the counsellor's stability, imperturbability, integrity and concern are what matters. When all is said and done, these perhaps are the qualities of the really first-class professional teacher who needs no system or organization to evoke from his students the respect he deserves or to exert the influence they recognize; who may select himself and be selected by others; who needs little training but requires more support than is currently available, and whose students know him to be what he seems to be.

Appendix
Children and Young Persons Act, 1969

Since this book was finished the first step towards implementing this Act has been taken. It is important to counsellors in schools, because it will have increasing effects upon clients whom they refer to outside agencies. It makes mandatory consultation between police and social workers when offences are committed by those under seventeen years of age, and gives statutory recognition to the cautionary role of Police Liaison Services.

For teachers, especially those who counsel or have pastoral duties, its real significance is that it recognises their social welfare role. It states in effect that co-operation between parents, teachers, social workers and police will solve, without recourse to the Courts, the problems of many children who are in any way deprived, in hardship, or have committed offences. The Courts may only be required to adjudicate where these consulting agencies cannot agree on a course of action about a given juvenile. Some time must elapse before the full effects of the Act work out in practice, but a study of it would be rewarding to interested teachers and counsellors, for it sets out to do what is best and appropriate for each child concerned.

For the great majority of their clients, however, it does not affect the work of counsellors or their use of referral, in the terms and under the conditions outlined in Chapter V.

Suggestions for further reading

GUIDANCE AND COUNSELLING

1. *Guidance and Counselling in British Schools*, H. Lytton and M. Croft (London, Edward Arnold, 1969)
2. *Teachers as Counsellors*, Alick Holden (London, Constable, 1969)
3. *Client-centered Therapy*, Carl Rogers (London, Constable, 1965)
4. *Counselling and Psychotherapy*, Carl Rogers (London, Constable, 1942)
5. *Counselling in Practice*, E. Jones (London, Ward Lock, 1970)

SOCIAL SERVICES AND CASEWORK

6. *Local Health and Welfare Services*, J. Parker (The New Town and County Hall Series: London, Allen & Unwin, 1965)
7. *Guide to the Social Services*, Family Welfare Association (address: Denison House, 296 Vauxhall Bridge Road, London SW1), 1969
8. *Social Casework*, E. H. Davison (London, Baillière, Tindall and Cassell, 1965)
9. *Authority in Social Casework*, R. Foren and R. Bailey (Oxford, Pergamon Press, 1968)
10. *The Caseworker's Use of Relationships*, M. L. Ferard and N. K. Hunnybun (London, Tavistock, 1962)

PSYCHOLOGY AND PHILOSOPHY

11. *Introduction to Jung's Psychology*, F. Fordham (Harmondsworth, Pelican, 1953)

12. *Between Man and Man*, Martin Buber (London, Fontana, 1961)

13. *The Divided Self*, R. D. Laing (Harmondsworth, Pelican, 1960)

14. *Development of Personality*, T. A. Ratcliffe (London, Allen & Unwin, 1967)

15. *The Family and Individual Development*, D. W. Winnicott (London, Tavistock, 1965)

16. *Introduction to the Philosophy of Education*, S. J. Curtis, (London, University Tutorial Press, 1965)

17. *The Moral Judgement of the Child*, J. Piaget (London, Routledge & Kegan Paul, 1960)

Index